Practical Software Engineering

The Addison-Wesley Object Technology Series

Grady Booch, Ivar Jacobson, and James Rumbaugh, Series Editors

For more information, check out the series web site at www.awprofessional.com/otseries.

Ahmed/Umrysh, *Developing Enterprise Java Applications with J2EE™ and UML*

Arlow/Neustadt, *UML and the Unified Process: Practical Object-Oriented Analysis and Design*

Armour/Miller, *Advanced Use Case Modeling: Software Systems*

Bellin/Simone, *The CRC Card Book*

Binder, *Testing Object-Oriented Systems: Models, Patterns, and Tools*

Bittner/Spence, *Use Case Modeling*

Booch, *Object Solutions: Managing the Object-Oriented Project*

Booch, *Object-Oriented Analysis and Design with Applications, 2E*

Booch/Bryan, *Software Engineering with ADA, 3E*

Booch/Rumbaugh/Jacobson, *The Unified Modeling Language User Guide*

Box/Brown/Ewald/Sells, *Effective COM: 50 Ways to Improve Your COM and MTS-based Applications*

Carlson, *Modeling XML Applications with UML: Practical e-Business Applications*

Cockburn, *Surviving Object-Oriented Projects: A Manager's Guide*

Collins, *Designing Object-Oriented User Interfaces*

Conallen, *Building Web Applications with UML, 2E*

D'Souza/Wills, *Objects, Components, and Frameworks with UML: The Catalysis Approach*

Douglass, *Doing Hard Time: Developing Real-Time Systems with UML, Objects, Frameworks, and Patterns*

Douglass, *Real-Time Design Patterns: Robust Scalable Architecture for Real-Time Systems*

Douglass, *Real-Time UML, 2E: Developing Efficient Objects for Embedded Systems*

Eeles/Houston/Kozaczynski, *Building J2EE™ Applications with the Rational Unified Process*

Fontoura/Pree/Rumpe, *The UML Profile for Framework Architectures*

Fowler, *Analysis Patterns: Reusable Object Models*

Fowler et al., *Refactoring: Improving the Design of Existing Code*

Fowler, *UML Distilled, 3E: A Brief Guide to the Standard Object Modeling Language*

Gomaa, *Designing Concurrent, Distributed, and Real-Time Applications with UML*

Graham, *Object-Oriented Methods, 3E: Principles and Practice*

Heinckiens, *Building Scalable Database Applications: Object-Oriented Design, Architectures, and Implementations*

Hofmeister/Nord/Dilip, *Applied Software Architecture*

Jacobson/Booch/Rumbaugh, *The Unified Software Development Process*

Jordan, *C++ Object Databases: Programming with the ODMG Standard*

Kleppe/Warmer/Bast, *MDA Explained: The Model Driven Architecture™: Practice and Promise*

Kroll/Kruchten, *The Rational Unified Process Made Easy: A Practitioner's Guide to the RUP*

Kruchten, *The Rational Unified Process, An Introduction, 2E*

Lau, *The Art of Objects: Object-Oriented Design and Architecture*

Leffingwell/Widrig, *Managing Software Requirements, 2E: A Use Case Approach*

Marshall, *Enterprise Modeling with UML: Designing Successful Software through Business Analysis*

Manassis, *Practical Software Engineering: Analysis and Design fo the .NET Platform*

McGregor/Sykes, *A Practical Guide to Testing Object-Oriented Software*

Mellor/Balcer, *Executable UML: A Foundation for Model-Driven Architecture*

Naiburg/Maksimchuk, *UML for Database Design*

Oestereich, *Developing Software with UML: Object-Oriented Analysis and Design in Practice, 2E*

Page-Jones, *Fundamentals of Object-Oriented Design in UML*

Pohl, *Object-Oriented Programming Using C++, 2E*

Quatrani, *Visual Modeling with Rational Rose 2002 and UML*

Rector/Sells, *ATL Internals*

Reed, *Developing Applications with Visual Basic and UML*

Rosenberg/Scott, *Applying Use Case Driven Object Modeling with UML: An Annotated e-Commerce Example*

Rosenberg/Scott, *Use Case Driven Object Modeling with UML: A Practical Approach*

Royce, *Software Project Management: A Unified Framework*

Rumbaugh/Jacobson/Booch, *The Unified Modeling Language Reference Manual*

Schneider/Winters, *Applying Use Cases, 2E: A Practical Guide*

Shan/Earle, *Enterprise Computing with Objects: From Client/Serve Environments to the Internet*

Smith/Williams, *Performance Solutions: A Practical Guide to Creating Responsive, Scalable Software*

Stevens/Pooley, *Using UML, Updated Edition: Software Engineering with Objects and Components*

Unhelkar, *Process Quality Assurance for UML-Based Projects*

van Harmelen, *Object Modeling: Designing Interactive Systems*

Wake, *Refactoring Workbook*

Warmer/Kleppe, *The Object Constraint Language, Second Edition. Getting Your Models Ready for MDA*

White, *Software Configuration Management Strategies and Rational ClearCase®: A Practical Introduction*

The Component Software Series

Clemens Szyperski, Series Editor

For more information, check out the series web site at www.awprofessional.com/csseries.

Allen, *Realizing eBusiness with Components*

Apperly et al., *Service- and Component-based Development: Using the Select Perspective™ and UML*

Atkinson et al., *Component-Based Product Line Engineering with UML*

Cheesman/Daniels, *UML Components: A Simple Process for Specifying Component-Based Software*

Szyperski, *Component Software, 2E: Beyond Object-Oriented Programming*

Whitehead, *Component-Based Development: Principles and Planning for Business Systems*

Practical Software Engineering

Analysis and Design for the .NET Platform

Enricos Manassis

✦Addison-Wesley

Boston • San Francisco • New York • Toronto • Montreal
London • Munich • Paris • Madrid
Capetown • Sydney • Tokyo • Singapore • Mexico City

The publisher offers discounts on this book when ordered in quantity for bulk purchases and special sales. For more information, please contact:

U.S. Corporate and Government Sales
(800) 382-3419
corpsales@pearsontechgroup.com

For sales outside of the U.S., please contact:

International Sales
(317) 581-3793
international@pearsontechgroup.com

Visit Addison-Wesley on the Web: www.awprofessional.com

Library of Congress Cataloging-in-Publication Data
Manassis, Enricos.
　　Practical software engineering: analysis and design for the .NET platform/Enricos Manassis.
　　　　p.　cm.
　　Includes bibliographical references and index.
　　ISBN 0-321-13619-5 (a;l. paper)
　　　　1. Software engineering. 2. Computer software—Development. 3. Microsoft.net
　　framework. I. Title.

QA76.758.M278 2003
005.1—dc22

2003057750

ISBN: 0-321-13619-5
Text printed on recycled paper
1 2 3 4 5 6 7 8 9 10—CRS—0706050403
First printing, September 2003

To my parents, for the education and values I received.

To Scott Weinberg, for showing me the path of continuous development.

Contents

List of Figures

Preface

Motivation

During the last several years I have had the opportunity to acquire and develop a variety of technical and nontechnical skills. Specifically, I focused on developing my skills in the following three aspects of software development:

- The process of engineering software-intensive systems: understanding *Who* is doing *What* and *When,* for the successful development of a software system. A successful system is a system that is completed on time, within budget, with controlled and measured quality, fulfilling all the requirements in a traceable way.

- Object-oriented analysis and design methodology, which is based on use case analysis and UML design. Though UML has proven to be a powerful notation with adequate semantics in order to represent object-oriented concepts, successfully modeling a system is really a matter of the practitioner's experience in translating use case specifications into meaningful object designs. This addresses the *How* in specific parts of the *What* of the process. Moreover, these designs need to be integrated at a detailed level within a specific technological platform.

- The technology, specifically the Microsoft Windows platform as an application server. I participated in the development of distributed systems, with COM and MTS initially, later with COM+ and now with .NET.

The insight I have gained from these experiences is that to be successful, modern software engineering has to integrate all three of these aspects. This is also reflected in the conceptual thread in the presentation of the above three elements: The *What* of the process has to translate into the *How* of the model, which in turn has to integrate the architecture of the technology used to implement the system.

At the same time I was very conscious of the very poor record of success (as defined above) of building software systems. I always wonder what our modern cities would look like if our civilization constructed buildings the way it constructs software. A lot of the people I met in the industry were lacking this consciousness, and my conclusion was that it was due to a lack of education in software engineering. Though myriad books already address the three elements listed above separately and in great detail, they rarely ever cover all the issues at the same time. In some cases the issues are covered in such fine detail that the reader misses the vision of the whole software engineering approach.

Goals of this Book

This book covers in one installment the three aspects of process, methods, and technology. Moreover and very importantly, it covers these issues in a concise and practical way. At the same time, this book focuses solely on the functional aspects of software development, limiting the scope of the software engineering discussion, but thoroughly exploring this aspect, which is of direct concern to the main stakeholders of any business automation solution: the business users. My approach is to describe the steps of the development process and the thought process that you need to follow to go from one step to the next, going all the way to the complete solution.

The book takes the point of view of a beginner or intermediate practitioner who is asked to develop an e-commerce system, using a rigorous approach to system specification, analysis, and design. One way to achieve this is to read an extensive array of specialized books, each describing a specific element of knowledge to acquire. This approach is time-consuming; by the time you're done you are an experienced practitioner. In contrast, this book aims to quickly give you a holistic vision of the issues involved and hence a better understanding of the process of applying a rigorous approach to software development. At the same time, you will find throughout this book a set of references to develop detailed knowledge of the topic at hand, thus giving you directions for deeper skill development.

The precise objective of this book is to present you with a holistic view of software development for distributed e-commerce systems. Spanning requirements analysis to design, implementation, and testing, it covers all aspects of a pragmatic approach to modern software engineering, leveraging the most current and recognized best practices.

Key features of this book include the following:

- Use of a case study. A specific functionality that is implemented in the sample application is used throughout the book as a conceptual thread to demonstrate all the process activities.

- Use of a holistic vision of process, method, and technology (.NET). This book presents hands-on object-oriented analysis and design and describes the thought process from requirements capture to class model and code generation. It presents a hands-on software development process (as an instantiation of a subset of the Rational Unified Process; see *The Rational Unified Process: An Introduction*). The process is supported by the book's structure itself.

- Show the forest (the concepts) behind the tree (the design of a sample application). This book provides references to explore in more depth the new concepts introduced in each section.

- Serve the knowledge in a way that unifies your understanding of technology with design and process. You gain insight without being overwhelmed by extended descriptions that try to cover every element of the technology (.NET), the methods (object-oriented analysis and design), and the process (Rational Unified Process).

Who Should Read this Book?

This book is aimed at a wide range of people involved in software development. The roles that will benefit the most are those who are the most closely related to development: developers, software architects, functional architects/analysts, testers, and project managers.

This book assumes that you have a basic knowledge of software development and an introductory understanding of object-oriented principles, use case analysis, and UML notation (a very practical book for understanding UML is *UML Distilled, Second Edition*). It also assumes basic knowledge of the .NET framework, specifically for understanding the design and implementation models, as well as for reviewing the companion code. Throughout the book you will find references to other books for further reading. All these references are summarized at the end of the book in the Practical Bibliography. This bibliography is a comprehensive set of resources that will enable you to delve even more deeply into the information presented here. These books, along with the appropriate hands-on experience, will help you achieve expertise in software engineering.

Structure of the Book

The structure of the book follows the lifecycle of a single iteration in the development of the system. This structure is consistent with the principles put forward by the Rational Unified Process, albeit simplified in order to achieve the objective of practicality. We can consider the structure of the book to be a vertical slice in the Rational Unified Process, where we examine the workflows that are most relevant to the development activities.

Chapter 1 will introduce some software engineering principles to get you into the correct mindset for a practical approach to a rigorous software development process. It will also introduce the case study that will be used throughout the rest of the book. Finally, it will present the software development process that will be followed, further underlined by the book's structure itself.

The rest of the book will take you through a case study for specifying, analyzing, designing, and implementing a sample software system on the .NET framework, using a simple and practical approach. The book is divided into two parts that address the two main areas of concern in the software development process: Part I is the system specification, and Part II is the system design. The separation also represents the point in the process where the user representatives stop their involvement in the production of development artifacts.

The structure of each chapter is organized as follows:

- The Introduction will review in some detail the concepts that will be discussed in the current chapter and will place the activities of the chapter in the correct context within the process. This is also where you will find most of the references to books that delve into the details of the methods presented in the chapter.

- The Approach describes the activity covered by the chapter. In this part you will find an introduction to the methods and techniques that will be applied to produce the artifacts. This book is not meant to cover the full details of the methods and techniques, so you will also find references for further reading in this section.

- The Case Study describes developing an artifact for that activity. In this part you will find a concrete application of the described method to the corresponding part of the overall case study.

- The Summary will stress the relationship of what you have seen in the chapter to the overall process. The strong elements of the applied technique are also pointed out.

Companion Site

The complete case study can be found at `www.booksreasy.com`. This is a demo site where you can work with the sample application that is featured in the book. You can also download the complete models for Rational XDE and the source code for Microsoft Visual Studio .NET. This application is useful in two perspectives:

- It is a concise and complete sample application that demonstrates a robust architecture for .NET systems, thus helping you acquire hands-on knowledge of .NET.

- It demonstrates the design of a .NET system using UML, round-trip engineering, and the integration of Rational XDE with Microsoft Visual Studio .NET. In this perspective, the book can be seen as a tutorial to the design of the companion .NET sample.

As a consequence, you can use all the material as a robust basis for your own development projects. I encourage you to download, review, and experiment with the material while reading this book.

For your convenience, enlarged versions of the sequence diagrams are available on Addison-Wesley's Web site: `www.awprofessional.com/titles/0321136195`.

About the Author

Enricos Manassis is a seasoned information technology consultant. With over 14 years in the field, he has acquired extensive experience in various roles in the whole software development lifecycle. From developer to tester, software architect, functional analyst, and project manager, Enricos has gained a holistic vision of software development and applying engineering principles to the process. His main role has been as a software architect on the Microsoft platform, with his current focus being the development of solutions on the .NET framework.

Enricos can be reached at or through the book's companion site, `Enricos.Manassis@BooksREasy.com`.

Acknowledgments

I would hereby like to express my special thanks to a few people without whose help and contribution I would never have been able to achieve this considerable undertaking.

Thanks to George Karavias, who was first to review the book project, but who also did the initial review of most of the book's content, correcting to the best extent my (perfectible) prose in English; and Yannis Manassis, for his suggestions on the project, early reviews, and the moral support through this exciting but demanding period.

Thanks also to Viki Williams, my editor, for believing in my proposed approach and promoting it in Addison-Wesley, as well as guiding me through this first attempt in authoring. By the same token I would also like to thank Mary O'Brien for promoting the book in the Object Technologies Series, and all the folks in editorial and production for contributing to a polished result.

Doing a good job on a book is also very much a matter of having the insightful contribution of a few very knowledgeable reviewers. Thanks to Anthony Kesterton from Rational Corporation UK for all his counseling and support before and during the work, as well as for his thorough review of the manuscript; and Professor Balbir Barn, Subject Head Computing at Thames Valley University (London), who kindly agreed to review the manuscript, sharing his considerable insight on the topics addressed. Double thanks to Philippe Kruchten for twice reviewing the material, once after the first draft and then after all changes and corrections were made.

Many thanks also to the guys at Neovera (`www.neovera.com`) for hosting and supporting the companion site.

—Enricos Manassis

Chapter 1

Introduction

What Is Software Engineering?

As its title indicates, this book is about software engineering. Thus, it is appropriate to introduce some definitions and describe some concepts of software engineering. This will also be useful in order to acquire the correct mindset and get the right perspective to better understand the rest of the material. Bear in mind, however, that, as presented in the Preface, the discussion focuses solely on the functional aspects of software engineering. In reality, the scope of the software engineering discipline is much broader than just the functional aspect, as you can discover by reviewing the documentation from the Software Engineering Body of Knowledge (SWEBOK; www.swebok.org). Nevertheless, this short introductory section focuses on the functional aspect. Though this section might look more like a philosophical discussion, my premise is that it will bring useful insight for the rest of the presentation.

Here is the working definition of software engineering that I will use, and which is most applicable to the discussion in this book. It is a definition in two parts, which are related and need to be considered as a whole:

- Refinement of knowledge through successive abstraction levels of representation.
- Traceability of each and every item of information between abstraction levels.

Abstraction Levels

The first part of the definition states that software engineering is about manipulating *knowledge*. Indeed, developing a software system is about expressing some knowledge somehow. It is about *refinement*, because the knowledge is taken from a high-level vision down to code and system configuration. This refinement is structured into *abstraction levels*, where on each level the knowledge is in the form of a specific set of representations. Note that when refining the knowledge there is an expected increase in the diversity of the types of its representation.

Figure 1-1 shows the structure of the abstraction levels. One important distinction made is the clear separation of the domain space and the solution space. The domain space deals with the description of the business and captures the knowledge of the business. This description exists independently of any automation solution that may be implemented in a specific organization. This knowledge is captured in business models and has to be maintained to accurately reflect the evolution of the definition of business functions and the related business processes. Capturing the knowledge of the business is also the prerequisite for any organization to move up on the ladder of the Capability Maturity Model.[1]

Note that in the literature you may find a slightly different wording for this duality, where the domain space is referred to as problem domain and the solution space as solution domain. I personally prefer and advocate the definition in this book, as it is more consistent with the everyday language spoken in the business world. Indeed, you will more often hear people speak of their business domain knowledge than about their business problem knowledge.

I also like to view the domain space in the two aspects of business functions and industries. Each organization is structured around a number of business functions that together collaborate to perform the business of the

---

1. More information on the Capability Maturity Model can be found at `http://www.sei.cmu.edu/cmm`.

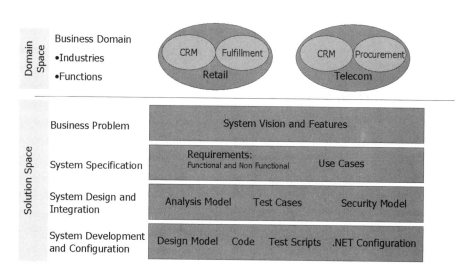

Figure 1-1: Abstraction levels.

organization. Examples of business functions are Customer Relationship Management (CRM), procurement, and fulfillment. Each organization is also a player within a particular industry, for example, Telecom, Retail, Banking, and others. Some business functions appear in every organization, irrespective of the industry they are part of.

It is interesting to note that while one business function is very likely to have a similar definition and terminology for all the organizations within one specific industry, the same business function may very well have a very different definition and terminology in a different industry. Moreover, within one specific industry, the more mature organizations are likely to have adopted a common definition and terminology for a specific business function. This awareness is important, as we will later consider the categorization of system features into business functions that may (or may not) be reusable, depending on the factors considered above. Appendix A, "Future Vision," shows you why this awareness is also particularly important for companies that produce prepackaged solutions for business functions.

In Figure 1-1, all the rest of the abstraction levels deal with the solution space. This is the business automation solution space, and it will be my main area of concern in this book.

I like to consider four levels of abstraction in the solution space. The *business problem definition* is likely to take the form of a system vision document, which documents a list of features. The knowledge at this abstraction level can be represented in a few pages of concise text. The *system specification* can be defined by the requirements and use case definition documents. This is where the refinement of the knowledge becomes clear. The knowledge representation (information) at the system specification level is obviously much more extended than at the business problem level. The knowledge continues to be refined through the *system design and integration* level to finally reach the *system development and configuration* level. At this level, the refinement of the knowledge is likely to have produced a huge amount of information, possibly in the form of millions of lines of code. The vision has turned into a solution, which automates a specific part of the business operations.

Traceability

Now let's consider the second part of the definition of software engineering, where we can find three concepts: *traceability*, *item of information*, and *abstraction levels*. These concepts connect the two parts of the definition in the following two ways:

- The concept of *knowledge* in the first part of the definition relates to the concept of *items of information* in the second part of the definition. An item of information "realizes" a piece of knowledge.[2] The concept of *item of information* is expressed throughout the book by the term "artifact."

- The concept of *abstraction levels* connects the two definitions by the means of *traceability*. Indeed, intuitively, we expect that the information items representing one abstraction level can somehow be connected to the information items of the next abstraction level. We have to view these

---

2. "Realization" is a word that will be used extensively throughout the text. Its meaning is defined by its usage within the UML language (e.g., a use case storyboard realizes a use case). A general definition of the verb, which accurately reflects the sense of its usage in this book, is "to bring into concrete existence."

connections as relationships of some sort that we have to formalize. Traceability is all about defining formalized relationships between the *items of information*.

Figure 1-2 shows information items of successive abstraction levels connected by arrows. These arrows define a relationship between two information items, which in turn represent the realization of knowledge at two successive levels of abstraction. These relationships represent the traceability of the information. What is very important to understand is that these relationships are not just arrows on a sheet of paper. Each of these relationships (i.e., each arrow) is "realized" by the means of a tool, method, or technique. Hence, each relationship represents a specific tool, method, or technique, which is defined by the software development process selected. The concept of traceability is central to this book, as through the chapters the discussion clearly presents the input and output artifacts of each stage of the process, and how they trace to each other by describing the thought process of going from the inputs to the outputs.

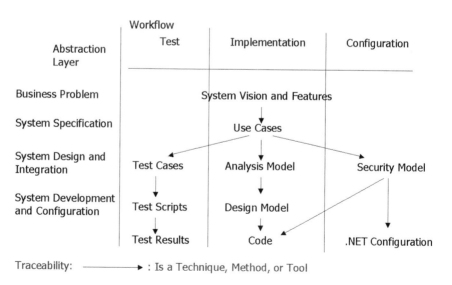

Figure 1-2: Traceability.

Practical Implications

The practical implications of the software engineering definition and the discussion above is that to achieve this vision we need to *implement* traceability between all the information items that will constitute a software automation solution. The means to implement traceability are

- Abiding by a clearly defined *process*.
- Describing a *technique* or *method* (e.g., use case analysis method or the technique of role-based security matrix, which you will see in Chapter 8).
- Using a *tool* (e.g., Rational XDE with Microsoft Visual Studio .NET) that enables automatic synchronization (hence tracing) of code to model, and the other way around.

By virtue of knowing and understanding these techniques, methods, or tools, you can relate all the information items produced in the course of a software development effort, with the ultimate goal being to demonstrate that the system does what it is meant to do. In other words, you can trace each and every feature the client wants, down to the system code and configuration. This ability defines a measure of functional coverage. Collectively, all this defines a measure of the quality of the system, which can now be measured in a very mechanical way, relying on the traceability of the items of information. And this is exactly the concept and vision of software engineering covered by the definition above.

The most prominent result of implementing traceability is the improved ability to execute impact analysis. It is easier and more accurate to identify the changes on any particular part of the system that will result from modifications in any level of system specification. In other words, when changing one artifact you can easily trace which other artifact(s) will be impacted downstream, down to the system code and configuration. Chapter 10 presents a case study that will demonstrate how traceability is put to good use in a situation where changes have to be made in the system specification, and how it preserves the quality of the solution.

Figure 1-3 completely covers the concepts found in the definition of software engineering. This is a schematic view in order to illustrate the concepts, while Figures 1-6 to 1-9 present a more precise and complete view, in depicting the practical process presented in this book. This process leverages

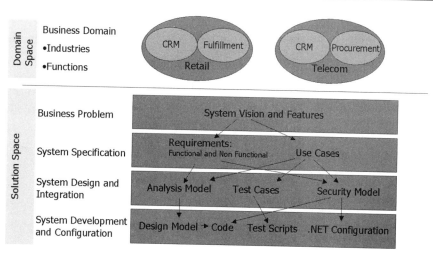

Figure 1-3: Abstraction levels and traceability.

the practical implications of the software engineering vision by appropriately using process and methods but also simple techniques and the capabilities of available tools.

The Case Study

The rest of this book will go through a case study of specifying, analyzing, designing, implementing, and testing a sample Web application for .NET. The application is a fictitious on-line bookstore named BooksREasy. Chapter 3 describes the features of this solution. There are six models produced as part of the process: business model, use case model, user experience (Ux) model, analysis model, design and implementation models, and database model.

The approach is to present you with a very simple but complete and comprehensive case study. The bookstore supports the whole buying experience from registration to login, browsing the catalogue, adding to the shopping cart, and checking out by paying with dummy credit cards. Using a simple case study ensures that all the artifacts produced during refinement are simple, and it is easier for you to review and understand the whole solution in a holistic way.

At the same time, you get a complete working system that can serve as the basis (code and model) for your own solutions. Note that this sample is itself an offspring of the Pearl Circle Online Auction, the companion sample of the Rational XDE tool. The example is simple enough that you can conceive simple extensions to help you exercise the concepts and approach presented.

This book will also be useful as a tutorial for the design of the features you want to implement. It will take you through the refinement of one feature: the registration of a new user. Because every feature can follow the same refinement process, there is no need for a more complex example. This refinement process reviews the lifecycle of a single iteration of the software development process—specifically, the iteration that supports the development of the user registration feature.

Finally, you should also note that the emphasis is on software engineering, which is why I will not show extensive code examples. You can use a tool like Rational XDE to generate a very precise code structure, specifically targeted for .NET. To achieve this, the tool needs to understand the underlying technological platform. Code examples will appear where the modeling technique is tightly related to the .NET technology. This is the case in the persistence framework, where the design takes advantage of the .NET DataSets. It is also the case for the design of role-based security, which takes advantage of .NET's corresponding security feature. All the code is available for download at www.booksreasy.com. Finally, bear in mind that this is not a book on .NET; I refer you to the numerous titles covering all aspects of the .NET technology.

The Process

To restate and summarize in a process-like perspective the vision introduced earlier, this book is really about demonstrating the process of the refinement of knowledge from a business automation vision, expressed concisely in a few pages of text, to a whole application, with all the artifacts involved in the process. It also demonstrates methods and techniques for ensuring the traceability of each and every artifact produced in the process. In this perspective, it will achieve the vision of the definition of software engineering put forward at the beginning of this chapter.

The book structure itself supports the underlying process. This process is a lightweight version of the Rational Unified Process (RUP), focusing on the development-centric workflows. A very good and practical book on this process is *The Rational Unified Process: An Introduction*. Though it is primarily the description of a software development process, RUP is also a tool that can be used by all members of a team involved in a software development project.

A core RUP concept is the notion of Guidelines. You can think of these as the tools and methods/techniques mentioned earlier in the definition of software engineering. In this way, RUP covers all aspects of the practical implications of this definition: process, tools, and methods/techniques. Rational has also developed a simplified version of RUP, the Rational Unified Process .NET Developers Configuration (RNDC), which also focuses on development-centric workflows. RNDC effectively complements the integration of the Rational XDE modeling tool with Visual Studio .NET, as it also references Microsoft Developer Network (MSDN) resources.

The process that I will present is inspired by practical considerations and reflects a hands-on, straightforward approach to development, while using a necessary and sufficient level of rigor to achieve the software engineering vision presented earlier. Consequently, similar to RUP but in a concise way, this book will cover all aspects of the practical implications of this vision. Figures 1-6 to 1-9 present a graphical view of the process and cover the system specification, system analysis and design, system implementation, and system testing.

An Iterative Process

As for the Rational Unified Process, the process presented integrates an iterative approach to software development. Table 1-1 shows the four phases of a RUP project lifecycle.

RUP also specifies that each phase is composed of one or more development lifecycles (each lifecycle defining one iteration). Table 1-2 shows the activities of a development lifecycle.

Figure 1-4 presents the way the project and development lifecycles relate to each other (this diagram can also be found in *The Rational Unified Process: An Introduction*).

Table 1-1: The RUP project lifecycle.

Phase	Main Activities
Inception	Business modeling
	Requirements capture
Elaboration	Requirements refinement
	System analysis and design
Construction	Refinement of the design
	Implementation
Transition	Test
	Deployment
	Configuration and change management

Figure 1-4 makes clear that for each phase of the project lifecycle, all activities of a development lifecycle will take place. Two development lifecycles from two different project phases will differ only in the relative proportion of the four development lifecycle activities. Figure 1-5 (which is also from *The Rational Unified Process: An Introduction*) represents this fact clearly. The core disciplines marked in bold will be the focus of this discussion: Business Modeling (marked in italics because it is not directly related to

Table 1-2: RUP lifecycle activities.

Activity	Main Artifacts
Requirements Analysis (Referred to as "System Specification" in this book)	Business model
	Use case model
Analysis and Design	Analysis model
	Design model
	Data model
	Role-based security matrix
Coding and Unit Testing	Implementation model
	Unit stubs
	Unit tests
Integration and Testing	Test cases
	Test coverage matrix

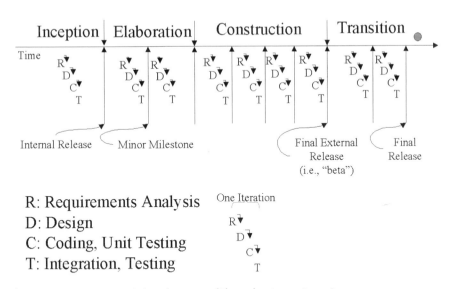

Figure 1-4: Project and development lifecycles in an iterative process.

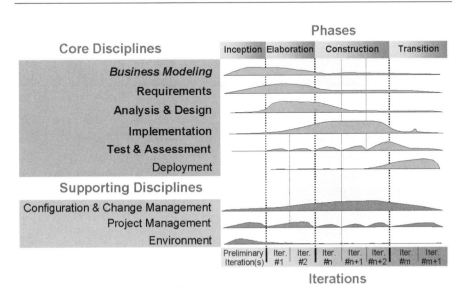

Figure 1-5: Distribution of effort for each activity during the project lifecycle.

development), Requirements, Analysis and Design, Implementation, and Test and Assessment.

The above discussion is a simplification of what is presented in RUP; I strongly encourage you to read *The Rational Unified Process: An Introduction* in order to get an accurate and complete understanding of these concepts.

This book focuses on development-centric activities, so I will not discuss the complete project lifecycle. Instead, I will consider a situation where a complete development lifecycle produces (from specification to code) one specific feature of the solution: the on-line registration of a new user. You can imagine yourself to be involved in a project where you will be playing all developer-centric roles through the project lifecycle.

The process diagrams that are pictured in the following sections present an artifact-centric vision of the process, depicting the dependencies between the artifacts. As such, it is important to understand that they do not imply a water-fall approach to software development. Any cohesive set of artifacts is likely to be used within a specific iteration (development lifecycle), though each of them may be produced and/or refined in different project phases (project life-cycle).

A practical implication of the above discussion is project planning, where you need to plan for architectural design activities even in the early stages of the project lifecycle, while focusing on system specification. Typically, the architectural design at this stage will involve the investigation and development of the architecturally significant mechanisms (as described in Chapter 6). Indeed, you do not need to have fully specified use cases in order to be able to design these mechanisms, which define the application infrastructure.

From the previous discussion it is clear that a complete development life-cycle for one development iteration would entail the following four areas of activities: system specification, system analysis and design, system coding, and system integration and testing. Because the focus of this book is on the func-tional aspects of system development, it will focus on the system specification and system design activities, while it skims through the system coding and system integration (and does not cover other activities like system deploy-ment). The specific integration of the testing activity in Chapter 9 focuses on the functional aspects of testing and covers an area that is often left out by developers. Indeed, Chapter 9 will first present the correct approach to testing, and then show how simple techniques can produce the correct test designs that will warrant the tracing of each test to a system use case (and permit a consistency check of the test coverage).

In the following sections I will give an overview of the various parts of the process, while presenting the relevant chapter where each part is discussed.

System Specification

The overall structure of the book defines two parts of the process, which represent two clearly separated concerns. In Part I, "System Specification," users are an integral part of the software development process and contribute to the definition of the various artifacts produced: business models and the vision document (obviously), but also use cases and the user experience model. They also decide the scope of the iterations. Part I also describes business process modeling activities, which are not an integral part of system specification, but present a complete and comprehensive approach to software engineering. Figure 1-6 presents an overview of the business modeling process, while Figure 1-7 presents the system specification part of the overall process. In these diagrams, as well as in Figures 1-8 and 1-9, all elements represent artifacts.

It is important to note that the process is defined by the artifacts and the activities that produce them. A solid line from an artifact A to an artifact B

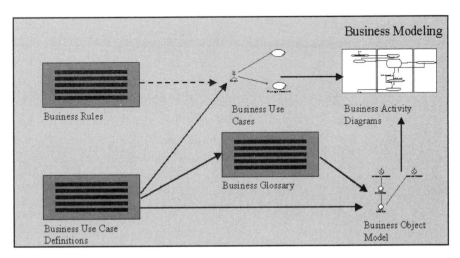

Figure 1-6: A practical process: Business modeling.

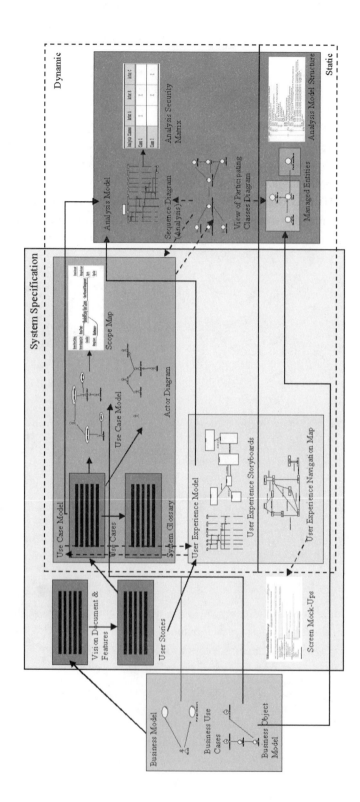

Figure 1-7: A practical process: System specification.

indicates that artifact A is a necessary input for creating artifact B. A dashed line indicates either an optional input artifact, or a situation where two artifacts (or sets of artifacts) need to be developed in parallel, each artifact feeding back in order to refine the other artifact (or sets of artifacts).

Chapter 2 considers business modeling activities, which result in the production of the artifacts presented in Figure 1-6, with their internal dependencies. This is the only chapter that is not directly relevant to development activities. As explained at the beginning of this chapter, business modeling activities and associated knowledge are not directly part of the solution space, which is my main concern in this book. Nevertheless, in this book, I am considering software development projects that aim to implement business automation solutions. The business requirements are thus the driving force of the system specification.

It is important to understand the starting point of the system development work, in order to put the rest of the process in context. This will help you gain a holistic vision of software engineering and also enable you to better communicate with the users who contribute to the system specification and who are focusing on the business implications of the solution you will be implementing.

There is at least one situation where business modeling occurs alongside system development. This happens when you do not yet have a model of the business for the specific function that is within the scope of the business automation solution. In that situation, you should also analyze the business function in order to model it, understand it, and possibly improve it, along with developing the corresponding automation solution. At the same time, this activity will bring a better understanding of the environment and the business in which the software will function. This will help create the best possible software for automating that business function.

Another important reason why it is useful to understand the business models is because they are documenting the glossary of the business. You should use this glossary when specifying the solution. Also, business modeling will produce the business object model, which will be used as the starting point for the static class model of the solution. Finally, the business model, along with the system requirements, will help identify an appropriate set of use cases. Because of the importance of the business glossary, business object model, and business rules artifacts for the rest of the process, teams should always carry out the activities involved in producing them, even in situations where there is no formal business-modeling phase defined.

Chapter 3 looks at how to specify the system requirements, starting with the system vision and features, as presented in Figure 1-7. This is the business problem definition, which is the highest level of abstraction in the solution space. It defines the scope of the business automation solution. We then refine the knowledge of the system vision and features into a list of requirements and use case definitions. Similar to RUP, the process followed is use case driven. As such, use case definition and use case analysis are both critical to the success of the solution.

The process presented defines two levels of use case descriptions. The first level is in the form of stories described by the users themselves: user stories. This is the same approach defined in Extreme Programming (XP), with the slight difference that in this book the user stories serve as the basis for the subsequent specification of the use cases. Read *EXtreme Programming EXplained* for more insight on that approach. After applying this approach to a few projects, I found it to be a very powerful and effective way to:

- Involve the users and give them a sense of ownership of the system.
- Get a head start on use case definitions.
- Serve as the basis for user experience discussions.
- Avoid a kind of paralysis that happens when users are not familiar with use cases and communication is difficult, especially when you interview them to get the information you need for the use case definitions.

The name of the artifact itself is carefully chosen to avoid any misconception from the users who are writing the use cases, thus giving you the leeway to mold the definitions into proper use cases, without any objections from the users. It is very important to note that the scope of this activity shall remain limited. Users are invited to write up, in simple terms and format, what they know of the related processes. Keep the schedule tight so users do not have the time to go into too much detail.

The user stories are used for two things: first for the use case model, then for the user experience model. From the user stories define a first draft of a use case model and use case descriptions. Then, in a second level of use case descriptions, the use cases are reworked with the users to a format more suitable for analysis. The diagram of actor relationships is carefully devised, as it is of critical importance to have a sensible model for the role-based security definition. The use case model is then produced. One thing to remember is that use case definitions and the use case model are the most important products of the system specification stage. In particular, use case definitions will be used as input to define test scenarios, driving the test artifacts (see further down in Figure 1-9).

The use case model is also the basic input for creating the so-called scope map, which is a diagram of all the identified use cases, organized in a hierarchy centered around business functions. This diagram helps prioritize the system features and allocate them into iterations. Note that the discussion revolves around functional requirements. Other types of requirements cover availability, reliability, manageability, performance, scalability, maintainability, and security. These nonfunctional requirements are also important and must be captured, but this book will not cover these concerns, in order to keep a limited and manageable functional scope that you can easily comprehend.

In Chapter 4 the user stories also serve as input to the definition of the user experience model, an activity that equally involves the users. This part is heavily inspired by RUP, though the discussion is kept concise and to the point. As presented in Figure 1-7, the screens identified from the user stories, and subsequently by reviewing the use cases, are organized into a series of navigation maps, which are diagrams of user experience model elements that represent the static relationships between the screens. The user stories, and subsequently the use cases, help create use case storyboards that describe the dynamics of the user interaction with the user experience model elements identified previously. You could also create screen mock-ups to attach to the screen definitions of the user experience model. The dashed arrows between the use case model and the user experience model indicate that you should use the information produced in one model to refine the artifacts of the other.

System Analysis and Design

In Part II, "System Analysis and Design," the software development team must find enough detail in the information produced in Part I to produce the rest of the artifacts, which will ultimately lead to the completed system. The development teams can use the artifacts produced during system specification as contracts for the implementation of the system. It is very important to understand that the separation of concerns does not mean a lack of communication.

And as much as the process is iterative, it is also very interactive. If attention and rigor have been applied in the system specification, you can expect to have very few incidents in the design and implementation stages where specifications are vague or inaccurate. Nevertheless, these incidents may occur, and in these situations you must go back to the corresponding system specification and review it with the users. This is also where traceability will play a major role. Each element of information at a specific level in the design should easily be traced to a specific element of information in the specification.

The next step in the process, presented in Chapter 5, is the development of the analysis model. As explained earlier, the overall process is divided into two main stages, system specification and system analysis and design (see Figure 1-8).

The analysis model, on the left part of Figure 1-8, is the first step in system design. It is an intermediary step that decouples the *What* of the system specification and the *How* of the system detail design, where the system will be modeled to the level of detail that will represent actual implementation classes. With the correct toolset, the design model can generate code in the appropriate language and technology. The main objective of the analysis model is to avoid the analysis paralysis phenomenon, which has been widely observed with teams using object-oriented analysis and design (OOAD) methods and UML for system design. Important points to keep in mind for the analysis model are the following:

- It serves as a decoupling of knowledge abstraction, between system specification and detailed design; that is, the analysis model can be seen as the output of system specification and the input to the design model.

- It is a high-level design model, which can be produced by either an analyst or a designer, without any emphasis on details. It's there to serve as a whiteboard to get a first cut of the responsibilities and attributes of the classes of the system. Still, it has to be designed with rigor, as we expect to identify most of the classes of the solution with their relationships.

- It serves as the glue between the use case model and the user experience model.

- Finally, it helps to control the completeness of the use case descriptions and model, specifically through the development of the View Of Participating Classes (VOPC) diagram. The central parts of the analysis model

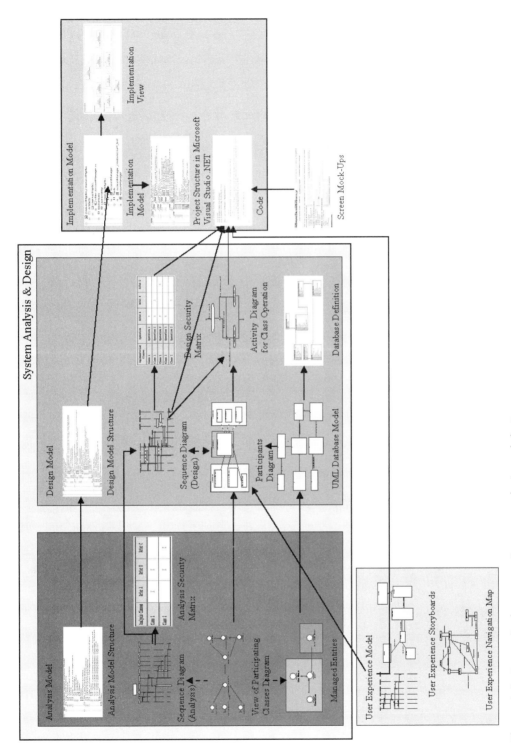

Figure 1-8: A practical process: System analysis and design.

are the VOPC diagram and the sequence diagrams that will help to make the first step in the detailed design.

The detailed design, pictured in the middle of Figure 1-8, is the next logical step in the process and is presented in Chapter 6. This part of the process is critical because it could lead to the generation of code. It is important to understand that, to achieve the software engineering vision defined earlier, you need to produce a complete design model. Along with analysis paralysis, this is the other plague of teams that use OOAD. Too often they stop short of creating a complete design model. The key input to the design model is the VOPC and sequence diagrams from the analysis model. The classes represented in these diagrams will all be part of the design model, with other classes possibly added to reflect the implementation details of the underlying technology used. In this book I will be using the .NET DataSets feature to implement data access.

Part of the detailed design stage is the development of a database model, which translates the key system entities relationships into a database model. Specifically, the approach will demonstrate the use of the UML Profile for Database Design. In the process presented, there is a lot of emphasis on the sequence diagrams that are considered core elements of the design model (and, for that matter, of the whole system design stage). These diagrams help identify the detail responsibilities of the implementation classes. An optional artifact in the design model is the activity diagram for class operations. These diagrams are useful to specify an algorithm or the flow of execution for a specific class operation.

In parallel, an important aspect of the design model is the model of the architecturally significant mechanisms. These are mechanisms that are of general use for the implementation of the functional features of the solution. They define the software infrastructure's application level, in contrast to its application server (.NET) or operating system (Microsoft Windows) level (which should not be represented in a model).

The final step, which relates directly to the production of code, is the implementation model (pictured on the right side of Figure 1-8). The related activities are presented in Chapter 7, which covers the practical implications of using modeling tools that integrate with integrated development environments. Specifically, I will demonstrate a set of best practices for the use of Microsoft Visual Studio .NET, from the perspective of the modeling techniques applied. With the implementation model we allocate the classes into physical containers. The type of container depends on the target technology used. For the .NET platform we will assign the classes into .NET assemblies. The implementation model will show us the dependencies between the assemblies, and this, in turn, will be used to configure the solution in Microsoft Visual Studio .NET. These dependencies will also impose the build order. Notice that this approach can trace the .NET configuration of the solution back to the model of the system.

Chapters 8 and 9 are not directly related to the production of code. Chapter 8 provides a lot of insight into using the role-based security feature of the .NET framework. This feature is often not used in an optimal way (or not used at all). This chapter shows an engineered approach to the role-based security design, and you will learn a simple technique to derive the configuration of .NET role-based security. This technique demonstrates the far-reaching consequences of the definition of software development given earlier. This technique should be part of a wider software development process, because the implementation of role-based security should be an activity of every software development for the .NET platform. There are two levels of role-based security modeling: analysis and design. The related artifacts are in the form of matrixes, which are produced at the corresponding stage of the process, as presented in Figure 1-8. These are the analysis security matrix and the design security matrix.

As much as security is a core concern for every system, testing is equally important. Chapter 9 focuses on functional testing; you will learn how to derive test cases from use cases. Again, this will demonstrate how traceability can be implemented in this crucial area of software development. You will see how a simple technique can assure you that all functions of the system have been covered with a test case. This in turn defines a rigorous way to measure the quality of the system, which is exactly what the software engineering vision defined earlier is meant to achieve.

Similar to role-based security, the test definition step should be part of a wider software development process, as every system has to undergo rigorous testing. In the same chapter you will also see how to track coverage of unit tests and how developing unit tests is a preliminary step to implementing the class operations. Figure 1-9 presents an overview of the process related to the functional testing activities.

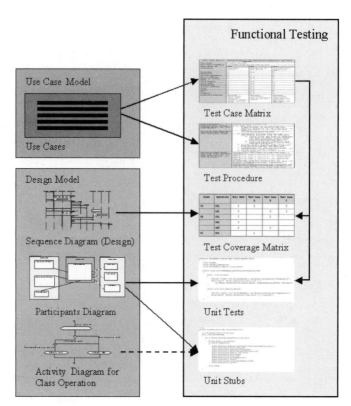

Figure 1-9: A practical process: Functional testing.

The presentation of a wider development process is not within the scope of this book, as the primary objective is to demonstrate basic software engineering principles (in particular, traceability). The process demonstrated is lightweight and hands on, covering the core objective of going from system vision to code. It is up to you to extend its use by "bolting on" every activity that you deem appropriate, as long as these activities maintain the traceability of each and every item of information between each stage of the process.

Roles in Software Development

As stated in the Preface, this book is of interest to all the software development roles, as the process presented demands the contribution of all. It is certain that each role will find a particular interest in the part where it contributes the most:

- Functional analysts, who in some organizations are named functional architects, will be interested in system specification, presented in Chapters 3 and 4. As a prerequisite they will also be interested in business modeling (Chapter 2) to understand its implications on system development. Also important for them is the development of the analysis model (Chapter 5), as well as system testing (Chapter 9). In reality, because the whole book focuses on the functional aspect of system development, functional analysts are likely to find interest in every aspect of the process.

- User interaction designers will be interested in understanding the system specification issues (Chapter 3) and developing the user experience model (Chapter 4), as well as the implications of the user interface and user experience on the overall system design.

- Software architects, or aspiring software architects, will be interested in every aspect of the process and will gain valuable insight on how elegant .NET systems can be produced by using a complete engineering approach.

- Developers/programmers will focus their interest on understanding the analysis model (Chapter 5), developing the design and implementation models (Chapters 6 and 7), modeling role-based security (Chapter 8), and testing—in particular, unit testing (Chapter 9). In reality, most of the developers will be interested in every aspect of the process, and by studying all the chapters they will gain valuable insight on object-oriented analysis and design and software development processes.

- Testers will be particularly interested in system specification (Chapters 3 and 4) and system testing (Chapter 9).

But, being hands-on, this book will benefit anyone playing any role in system development as described in the Rational Unified Process. It will bring valuable insight into what kind of deliverable is expected from their role, how each role integrates with other roles, and what other roles do within the process. The structure of the chapters (Introduction, Approach, Case Study, and Summary) is very helpful in this perspective, as it enables each role to delve more or less deeply into the contributions of other roles. At the least, every role, including the ones mentioned above, should read the Introductions and Summaries. Other roles that do not directly contribute to the activities developed in this book, but will also benefit by reading it, include the following:

- Business analysts will benefit, especially if they have not yet had the opportunity to work within the framework of the Rational Unified Process. Note, however, that although Chapter 2 describes business modeling, it does not delve into sufficient detail to be practically used by a business analyst. It is more useful for functional analysts to help them understand the inputs to their activities.

- Project managers will gain insight into how all the roles collaborate at the technical level, as well as the practical implication on project planning of using the process.

Part I

System Specification

Chapter 2
Business Model

Introduction

The Introduction to this chapter aims to set the scope of the business modeling activity that this book will cover. As mentioned in the Introduction to Chapter 1, business modeling is not directly related to development activities. At the same time, you must recognize the importance of business models as input for the development of high-quality software systems. The main concern of this book is with business automation solutions. But the business is what really defines the requirements for any information system. It defines the context in which the solution will operate. Therefore, we need a way to ensure that the system we are developing is correctly supporting the business functions and processes it is meant to automate. Intuitively, to achieve this we expect to have an accurate description of the business processes and function of the organization, in an appropriate format.

Unfortunately most organizations have documented only a partial description of their business procedures. Moreover, they seldom keep the documentation updated with the continuous evolution of the procedures. Obviously the bigger and more mature organizations often do a better job at documenting and maintaining their procedures, and this is of utmost importance in order to move up the ladder of organization maturity (see the discussion in Chapter 1 on the Capability Maturity Model).

In general, most organizations have textual descriptions of their procedures. But there is another approach that consists in documenting the business processes in UML using business extensions. This chapter is not by any means intended to be a detailed and exhaustive approach to business modeling. For more information you must read a specialized book on the topic, such as *The Object Advantage—Business Process Reengineering with Object Technology* (note, however, that this book does not use UML, as its publication predates the advent of UML). In contrast you will find in this chapter a presentation of business modeling using the current UML notation for this activity. Another in-depth book on the topic, which uses the UML notation for business modeling, is *Business Modeling with UML: Business Patterns at Work*.

The actual objective of this chapter is to introduce the business modeling activity and the artifacts produced, which are an important input for the system specification activities. In this chapter you will find, presented in a simple and practical way, the business modeling of one business function: customer management. This chapter will specifically focus on one part of this business function: the registration process. In subsequent chapters you will find how this business function is specified for automation and how you can use the business model to get a head start for the requirements and analysis and design workflows.

When reading this chapter, it is important that you keep in mind the way that the business model feeds into the system specification activities:

- To facilitate discussions. A business model creates the common definition and terminology needed for communication between the various roles (stakeholders) within an organization: management, business analysts, business designers, and business users at all levels. As such, the business models will help you, the software system developer, empathize with your business clients/users. The business model will give you the glossary to use for the system use case definitions.

- To find functional requirements. The business model is used as a basis to identify the correct set of system use cases that the system should implement to support the business function and process.

- To find nonfunctional requirements. These requirements, such as availability, reliability, manageability, performance, scalability, maintainability, and security, typically span the entire system. They are often generic and not attached to a specific system use case. This book will not focus on this aspect of system specification.
- To act as a basis for analysis and design of the system. The business object model can be used as the basis for the system class model. This mapping provides a starting point for the requirements and analysis steps. However, we will need more refinement, and you have to remember that the business object model is not sufficient to define the system class model.

Approach

As introduced in the overview, in the scope of this book the business process modeling activity is not meant to be a thorough and complete analysis of the business model. Rather, the aim is to exemplify the type of information that can be gathered at that level. You must also keep in mind that the business modeling work presented is more directly relevant to a context of information processes, which are processes that manipulate information (as opposed to production processes involving the manipulation of goods).

The perspective you have to take when creating this model is that it will capture business concepts, independently of any possible system that would implement these concepts. The concepts that we deal with are business actors (e.g., customer management) and business entities (e.g., a user account or an order). Business processes include not only the automated parts of the business but also (more importantly) the nonautomated parts of it. After all, you're doing business modeling because you are in the process of either automating an existing manual business function, or developing a new business function that will be automated directly. The following elements are very important in gaining the right mindset to approach this part of the modeling:

- Think of the business as being totally based on manual processes.
- Take the view of the customer (internal or external).
- Remember that business use cases deal with the concepts of the business while system use cases deal with the concepts of the system under development.

Business Modeling Artifacts

The business modeling activity will produce six artifacts: business use case definition, business use case model, business activity diagrams, business object model, business rules definitions, and business glossary.

The business use case definition is a document listing all the business use cases with their textual description.

The RUP specifies two UML models for business modeling:

- Business use case model: Describes business processes from an external perspective.
- Business object model: Describes business processes from an internal perspective.

Note that the business object model captures the business entities and their relationships at the business concept level, but can be used to drive a data-centric modeling approach (hence the internal perspective). Historically, this is how systems have been designed, but modern software development processes like RUP, and by extension the process presented in this book, promote a use case-driven approach (hence an external perspective).

The business rules definition will take the format of a document with each business rule listed (along with the business use cases where it is applicable). Another way to represent the business rules is within the business use case model using the Object Constraint Language (OCL); see *The Object Constraint Language* for a detailed description of how to use OCL to describe business rules. It is important to be aware that the business rules have to be traceable down to the system use cases, which will need to implement them. One business rule may be implemented by one or more use cases, while each use case may implement more than one business rule. However, some business rules appear just as constraints on the definition of the business objects in the business glossary. As you will see in Chapter 3, business rules are useful to identify alternate paths in system use cases. Not all business rules will define alternate paths, but you should carefully review the business rules definitions to get a head start on alternate paths, as well as achieve completeness in identifying them.

The business glossary defines the common terminology used within the organization when describing the business functions and processes. This glossary should also be used for the system specification activities.

Activity diagrams are a very important and powerful way to represent the workflows within a business process. Business processes often define a lot of parallel activities because, as you might expect, organizations strive to use their resources efficiently. Activity diagrams are very good at describing situations with parallel activities. While textual representation of a business use case document may be sufficient for workflows with a simple structure, when workflows start getting complex, activity diagrams are the best way to:

- Visualize the complexity of the workflow.
- Ensure that the workflow is complete.

Here is an important remark on traceability. The above approach promotes the use of six artifacts. It is obvious that there is duplication in the representation of the knowledge between some of these artifacts. Specifically, the business use case definition document represents knowledge in a textual format, while the business use case model represents the same knowledge in UML (that is, a graphical format). The same remark is applicable to the business rules document, which represents knowledge in textual format, while the business use case model can represent the rules attached as OCL to the model.

To achieve traceability, it is obvious that you have to maintain the knowledge in these two formats. But your work can be simplified and the traceability achieved automatically, if you use an appropriate modeling tool that supports the annotation of the use case model with the business use case definitions. The tool might also be able to generate textual reports of the definition that will then represent the knowledge in a textual format. This way, the textual representation of the business use cases does not need to be maintained, as it can be generated at will.

Business Modeling UML Elements

In RUP, business models are comprised of several stereotyped UML elements:

- Business actor represents a role played in relation to the business by someone or something in the business environment.

- Business use case defines a set of business use case instances; each instance is a sequence of actions a business performs that yields an observable result of value to a particular business actor. This definition emphasizes how a business process delivers value to the customers. This customer-centric perspective helps you conceive an external view of the business.

- Business worker represents an abstraction of a human or system that acts within the system. A business worker interacts with other business workers and manipulates business entities while participating in business use case realizations. In the next stage of the process, system specification, business workers that will not be automated will represent system actors in the use case model.

- Business entity represents conceptual objects that a physical customer will exchange with the organization (or which are exchanged within the organization). Typically, in the context of information processes, we can think of business entities as paper forms. Business entities are especially important, as they will define the basis for the entity classes, which will be created in a software solution.

- Business use case realization describes how a particular business use case is realized within the business object model, in terms of collaborating business workers and business entities. It is most common to use activity diagrams to represent the business use case realization. This approach has the advantage of enabling you to use swimlanes, which are coupled to the business actors and business worker classes in the business object model.

- Organization unit is a stereotyped UML package element, which is used to represent a business function.

Note that activity diagrams are also used to document program flow; you will see an example in Chapter 6 where it will be used to refine class operations. Within the activity diagram, you can show activities (sequential and parallel), actor or worker responsibility for an activity (with swimlanes), and the relationships and dependencies between activities.

Case Study

As stated in the Introduction, in the case study you will follow the refinement of one feature of the solution, from the business model to code. This feature is the registration of a new user account. Intuitively we can understand that, from a business perspective, it is sensible to be able to identify and manage the information related to our customers. Every organization has some kind of customer management business function. Figure 2-1 shows a simple categorization of the business functions defined for the case study. As a general remark, all UML elements used to represent business stereotypes are drawn with a small slash line in the lower right part of the icons. Each business function is presented with a stereotype of "organization unit" from the UML element of package.

Business Use Cases

Within the customer management business function we can expect to find a process related to registering a customer. We can also expect to find a process that enables the customer to modify personal information or demand that information be deleted. We thus identify a business actor whom we name Buyer and two business use cases, Register and Manage Account. Figure 2-2 presents a UML diagram that describes this situation.

The first activity you will be involved in when doing business modeling is to write a textual definition of the business process. In doing so you have to remember that you are describing a manual process. Table 2-1 shows the definition for the Register process. Note that we make the assumption that during the process there is also verification of the validity of the credit card. This is a bit contrived and unlikely to happen in the real world (where the credit card validation will happen only during checkout, at the time when some goods are

Customer Management   Store

Figure 2-1: Organization units.

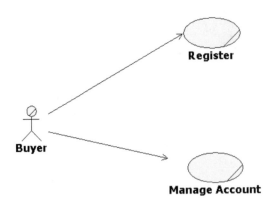

Figure 2-2: Business use cases for customer management.

ordered). In our case study we will be validating in both situations, as this will help illustrate some interesting concepts when defining the system use cases in Chapter 3.

Business Object Model

This simple definition will serve the purpose for the subsequent discussion. Reading through the description, you can identify a certain number of concepts that you need to define in an appropriate representation. The business actor who is involved in this business use case is named Buyer and has already been documented in the UML business use case model. The business workers involved are Customer Management and Credit Card Handling. You can also identify two business entities, User Account and Credit Card. The business workers and business entities need to be defined in the business object model, as in Figure 2-3. There are two different stereotypes used in these UML diagrams: Business workers are represented with a stick figure in the center, and business entities are represented as an underlined circle.

The business object model is there to convey the relationships between business objects (business workers and business entities). The only relationships that are relevant for a business object diagram are association, aggregation, and generalization. Keep in mind that this is not a class diagram;

Table 2-1: The registration process.

Business Use Case	Description
Register	The Buyer contacts Customer Management and requests to be registered with the organization.
	Customer Management gives the Buyer a form requesting User Account information.
	The Buyer fills in the form and turns it back. Customer Management:
	1. Verifies that the information is valid User Account information.
	2. Verifies that the information defines a new Buyer.
	3. Requests from Credit Card Handling to verify the validity of the Credit Card.
	If the information is valid, Customer Management can create a new User Account.
	Then, Customer Management informs the Buyer of the outcome of the request:
	■ The registration is completed and the acknowledgment conveys the account information as filed in the bookstore organization.
	■ Some invalid information was supplied and the acknowledgment conveys the reason why the registration failed. In this case it is up to the Buyer to initiate a new registration request.

therefore, we do not need to specify more precisely the relationships between the business objects. The entity objects in the business object diagram are especially important. These entity objects and their associations represent what is called the domain model. This is the static model of the business. The business entities can be used as the starting point of the entity model during the analysis and design of any software solution pertaining to the same domain model. Remember from the Introduction that the business model exists independently of any business automation solution.

Business Glossary

All of the business elements identified above should also appear in a business glossary document. Each element in the business glossary will be defined with

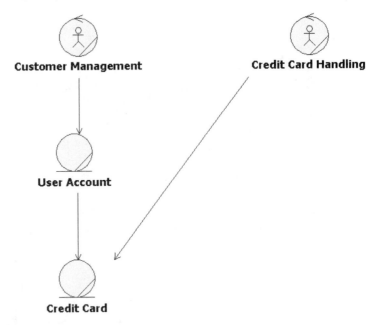

Figure 2-3: Business object model.

any appropriate attributes. In the registration example above, the description does not disclose what information is needed for the User Account. This will appear in the business glossary in the definition of a User Account. Table 2-2 is an excerpt of the business glossary for our small business example. This business glossary is complete relative to the Register business use case definition above.

Business Rules

Finally, the business definitions need to be completed with a repository of business rules. In the Register business use case definition, we can understand that invalid User Account or Credit Card information is a possible cause for the failure to create a new account, but we must have a way to specify other conditions that must be met during the registration process. A very simple example is that we do not want to accept two registrations from the same

Table 2-2: Business glossary excerpt.

Term	Definition
Buyer	Buyer is a bookstore user who places orders for books.
Credit Card	Credit Card information includes the following: ■ Name on account ■ Credit card type ■ Credit card number ■ Card expiration date Credit Card information is maintained as part of User Account information.
User Account	The User Account represents a person or an organization that has created an account with the bookstore. The User Account information includes the following: ■ Username (must have more than 8 alphanumeric characters, must contain no spaces, and must be case-insensitive). ■ Password (must have more than 8 alphanumeric characters, can contain spaces, and must be case-sensitive). ■ E-mail address. ■ Billing address. See Credit Card information.
Customer Management	Customer Management represents the roles and systems in BooksREasy that support the Customer Management business function
Credit Card Handling	Credit Card Handling represents the roles and systems in BooksREasy that process all credit card-related activities and operations: validate credit card, debit credit card, etc.

person. We must then specify the conditions when two sets of User Account information are considered to be the registration of the same buyer.

At the same time it is important to relate the business rules with the business use case(s) where they are applicable. The reason for this is to be able to trace the business rules to the system use cases where they are implemented. How is this possible? The business use cases define the business workers who participate to achieve the corresponding business process. For each business worker and for each business use case it participates in, you can define a candidate system use case. This can give you a useful starting point and consistency check when defining system use cases, but ultimately you have to exercise your own practical judgment.

Because of this, and in order to facilitate the tracing of the business rules to the system use cases, we need to attach them to the business use case(s) where they are applicable. To do so, the business rules will be defined with an attached list of references to the business use cases where they are involved, as presented in Table 2-3.

Business Activity Diagrams

Before the business modeling effort is considered complete, we need to design the UML activity diagrams for the business use cases. As mentioned in the Introduction, the best approach is to use partitioned activity diagrams with swimlanes. Each swimlane will represent either a business actor or a business worker.

Figure 2-4 presents the activity diagram for the Register business use case. In the Register business use case we can see from the business object diagram that there are two business workers involved: Customer Management and Credit Card Handling.

For the Register process of the case study, the workflow is very simple; you may think that an activity diagram is overkill. But using activity diagrams consistently helps you understand quickly and completely the business workflow documented. Thus, it is important to systematically produce this type of diagram.

Table 2-3: Business rules definitions.

Business Rule	Definition	Applicable Business Use Cases
Only One Registration per Buyer	A Buyer can only be registered once. If the Username in the User Account information is already on file, reject the request for registration.	Register
No Offending Words	The information entered by the user at any stage must not contain any word that appears in the organization's official list of offending words.	All

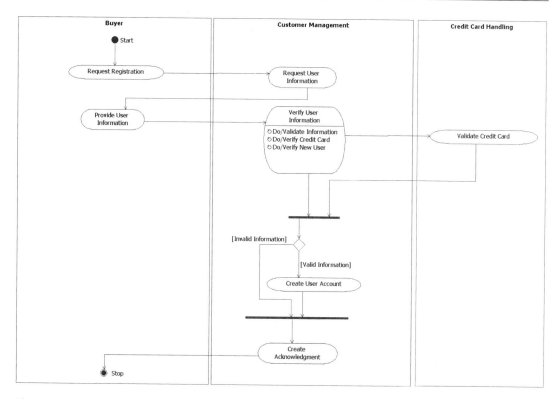

Figure 2-4: Activity diagram for the Register business use case.

Summary

In this chapter we reviewed the business modeling activity, which should ideally take place independently of any software development project. The reality is that in many organizations, a software development effort will be the opportunity to document the corresponding business processes of the organization. It is thus useful for you to understand and be prepared to participate in this activity.

In this activity, you produce six artifacts: business use case definition, business use case model, business activity diagrams, business object model, business rules definition, and business glossary. All together, these artifacts constitute the business function definitions and the terminology of the business where the organization operates.

The business use cases—along with the business workers—can suggest what the system use cases will be. Business rules have to be traced to system use cases; that is why they need to be attached to business use cases. Business rules may suggest alternate flows in system use cases.

The business entity associations define the domain model. This will be used directly as the basis for the system class model, the model that defines the persistent classes.

The business glossary should be used throughout the software development as the source of terminology for all artifacts produced.

Activity diagrams are the best way to describe business processes workflows. They ensure a complete and holistic understanding of the most complex workflows.

Chapter 3

System Requirements

Introduction

If you take a dozen practitioners involved in software development and ask them what they understand about Software Requirements Capture, you are likely to end up with a dozen different answers. In this chapter we will first define a comprehensive set of requirement artifacts and how they relate to each other, and then we will examine how these artifacts are produced in the context of our case study (and review examples of each of them). Again, all this material is largely compatible with RUP, although you will find one or two artifacts that are specific to the approach taken in this book.

Simply stated, the objective of capturing system requirements is to specify *What* the system will do. To achieve this objective we need to make sure that we can capture the real needs of the business users. To do so we have to identify these business users first and then describe their needs. These will be referred to as "stakeholder needs."

A stakeholder need is a business domain consideration; you have to think of it from the business domain perspective. You have to ask which people will really gain from investing in a new software system. You have to think of the stakeholders as people who are not aware of the intricacies of the technology but who understand the issues of the business. Not everyone thinks of a problem in terms of issues, but this is a very powerful mindset to acquire, because it is very easy to express needs if you think in terms of issues.

As a general note on the terminology used in the text, when using the term "use case" in this and the following chapters, I implicitly refer to "system use case," in contrast with the term "business use case" that was used in Chapter 2. You will specifically find the term "business use case" when I need to refer to that concept in the discussion.

Approach

System Vision and Features

Software engineering is all about refining knowledge. This is also what we will be doing in capturing system requirements. The first level of abstraction is the vision document; this has to be driven by the key stakeholders of the software development effort, in the form of a high-level document, which describes the solution in a few pages of text. The people who will write this document understand the business domain of the solution. In this document, it is useful to represent the following elements of knowledge:

- An executive summary of the solution. In any mature organization there will always be one single person who will have the overall responsibility for a business automation solution. It is desirable to involve this person in the deliverables of the solution, by ensuring that at least an executive-level description of the solution is under their responsibility. This will also ensure that the project has the appropriate executive backing and commitment.

- A high-level description of the problem that the system will address. This description can represent the list of business issues involved. Because businesspeople write the document, we are ensured that these issues will be expressed in business terms.

- The list of stakeholders and users of the system, with their descriptions and their concerns and responsibilities, which define their own personal perspective of the solution.

- A list of the features of the system, expressed in business terms. This part is central to the vision document. Indeed, a list of features is the most natural approach for people to express what a system must do. We can define a feature as a service the system provides, which supports one or more stakeholder needs. Features are an important intermediate step between the *What* of the specification and the *How* of the design. They can be seen as a high-level expression of the solution. Features are expressed in natural language that uses terms understood by all the stakeholders. If a feature is not understood by a stakeholder, this is an indication that it is expressed in overly detailed, specific terms and we have to restate it in more abstract, business terms. The feature list is also important because it defines the high-level view of the system scope.

- If there are specific constraints related to how the solution expresses the reality of the corresponding business domain, they must also be captured in business terms within the vision document.

- Finally, the vision document must describe any nonfunctional constraints relating to the way the solution will integrate and operate within the overall enterprise environment, including any constraints on development standards and processes of the organization. Examples of constraints include design requirements, limitations in cost or resources, and people skills development.

Note that a vision document has an important function of defining the high-level scope of the solution. In this perspective the content should be of practical applicability and not just a document for the sake of producing paper. Keep in mind that this goal of the vision document to specify the scope of the solution will ensure that this document is truly useful as a business-level system specification.

A final, but important, remark on the vision document is related to the situation where a business automation solution is developed in an organization where the business model has already been defined. In that situation, the functional objectives and scope of the solution can easily be defined relative to the business use cases or structure (organization units). The vision of the system must focus on the nonfunctional constraints as defined above. For the remainder of this book we will make the assumption that the organization has already defined a business model of the processes, which the solution studied will automate.

User Stories

In Chapter 1, I noted that the process presented is use case driven. That means that the use cases will be the reference for defining the functional requirements, describing the required behavior with precision and without any ambiguity. At the same time the use cases should not dictate in any way how the system will be designed. Technically, a use case describes a sequence of actions, performed by a system, which yields a result of value to the user.

A very simple, quick, and from my experience very effective technique to speed up and facilitate use case definitions is using what Extreme Programming (XP) calls user stories. You might consider using this technique as an intermediate step before detailing the use cases. It is especially helpful in situations where the users are not experienced in working with use cases. This activity can take the form of a half-day workshop; it entails asking the representatives of the user community to quickly write up what they expect the possible interactions of the various users with the system will be. Get a consensus on a number of areas to cover, representing use cases, and allocate each area to those who are not comfortable with each other, then get them to write up a story. User stories will be the prime input to define use cases.

The biggest issue that you will have to address in this step has to do with the so-called "granularity" of the use cases. A use case should not be too long (describing too much system behavior), nor too granular (not specifying a complete user task). A good approach is to consider the mental task model of the user: How do the users categorize the tasks they are assigned to do? Talking with the user representatives will help you identify a first cut for the set of user stories, and hence also use cases.

Note that using this approach has the practical implication that user stories can be used directly as input for creating the user experience model. Indeed, as you will see in Chapter 4, the correct mindset in order to create the user experience model is to consider the mental task model of the users. Users are not allowed to use any formatted templates. They have to write just plain text and include section headings (which are likely to correspond to use case names). Users also need to attach a description of the actors who will be interacting with the system.

The important point to remember is to not give the users too much time to write, as there is a risk that they will start thinking of too many details on how the system will work, instead of concentrating on what they expect of the system. The user stories are a throwaway artifact and should not be maintained. The important points to remember about user stories are that they are optional and they are created by the users themselves as a first draft of use cases; thus, they are not in an appropriate format for use case analysis. You will use them as input to write proper use case definitions.

Use Case Model and Actors

After the user stories have been produced, you can leave the users for a moment and integrate the information you know from the various artifacts produced so far: business use case model, business object model, vision document, and user stories. This work will result in a first draft of the use case definitions and the use case model, including the diagram of system actors. Note that, in parallel, you can use the same information to produce a first draft of the user experience, as we will review in the next chapter.

An alternate approach is to have a brainstorming session with the users to derive a list of detail requirements, the Requirements List; you are likely to end up with a huge number of items on the list. Having established the list, you have to rework it into functional and nonfunctional requirements. After defining an initial set of use cases, you must allocate each functional requirement to one or more use cases. All requirements have to be allocated. In this book I present the approach based on user stories, which has the advantage of being more useful in producing the user experience model.

The UML elements involved in the use case model are

- Actor, a role played by any person or system that is external to the system under development but interacts with it.
- System use case, which defines the sequence of actions that describe the interaction between the actors and the system for a specific function.

To define the initial set of use cases you will be using the information from the user stories, the business use case model, and the business object model. But there are no hard rules, and you must use practical judgment and your experience. Use the approach described above as a guideline for identifying user stories. When defining the draft use cases, you will be reworking the information found in the user stories and presenting it in a more formal way, using a use case template. A very powerful way to comprehend the use cases of the system is to represent them in a series of UML diagrams, which together with the use case definitions form the use case model. The use case model is the synthetic view of the functionality of the system. The objectives of this model are to:

- Produce some diagrams that represent the actors and their relationships (actor diagrams).

- Produce some diagrams that represent the use cases with the actors and their relationships (use case diagrams).

- Organize the use cases into packages that map to the conceptual categorization of the system functions.

It is important to maintain a precise model of the actors and their relationships by representing the actors and their relationships in one or more UML diagrams. More often than not, teams overlook the importance of a good model of the actors. Modeling the role-based security in Chapter 8 will give you the measure of the importance of having a good actor model.

Scope Map

When you have the first draft of the use cases and the use case model, you can review them with the users and prioritize the work based on the relative importance of the use cases. This is where you will define your development iterations. The overall idea is to be able to demonstrate progress in regular intervals (say, six-week intervals). At the end of each development iteration you should have a complete working system that covers an expanding set of use cases. Because it is most natural for people to organize information into hierarchies of categories, the best approach to help decide which use cases are the most important, and should therefore be developed in priority, is to structure the use cases into a hierarchy of use case packages. This organization conceptually defines a scope map, and it is very helpful to grasp the extent of the scope of the system. One package in the hierarchy defines a set of related use cases that should be developed within one iteration.

When organizing use cases into packages, you should strive to give a conceptual sense to the packaging you apply. An effective approach is to organize the use cases into "Business packages," thus regrouping the use cases that contribute to the realization of a specific business function. Bear in mind, though, that a use case may span more than one business function. In this situation use your best judgment to assign the use case to the most relevant Business package.

Use Cases

The next step is to refine and develop the use cases of the first iteration (and subsequently the use cases of the following iterations until completion of the solution). Having produced your first draft of use cases and the use case model, the hard work of system specification is now commencing. It is all about defining the use cases in every detail and without any ambiguity, as well as defining the actors and their interaction with the use cases. As introduced earlier, use cases are the central part of system specification; as such, the work of defining them is critical.

As described in Chapter 2, the business rules identified in business modeling will be useful to help identify alternate paths in the use cases. Not every business rule will result in an alternate path, but it is important that every business rule documented in the business rules table be traceable, in some way, to a use case.

Note that, in parallel, you will develop the user experience model, and you should use both the use case model and the user experience model to validate the consistency of the other.

While developing the use cases, you should also extend the business glossary. The catch is that you might need to create glossary entries for concepts that are pertaining to the system and not to the business. Remember from the previous chapter that we separate the concerns: business models deal with concepts of the business, while system models deal with concepts of the system in development.

An effective approach to this dilemma is to create a second glossary, the system glossary, where you will define all system-related concepts. Also note that you might in fact discover that some business concepts have been missed, or have been inaccurately defined in the business glossary. In that case, you must take the opportunity to update the business glossary. But for the system specification, you will need to use both glossaries.

Note that at this stage the test design effort should already have started, and the test strategy defined. As soon as the use cases are defined, test designers should start identifying the most appropriate test scenarios, and from these the test cases. This is also where analysts get very involved with test design. Testing will be discussed in detail in Chapter 9. Interestingly, the test scenarios identified by the test designers will also be used to identify which sequence diagrams need to be developed in analysis and design models, as we will see later in Chapters 5 and 6.

It is useful to define a use case template, as it brings structure to your thinking when describing the use cases. It is well known that use case templates tend to go wild, and teams put everything and anything in them. To define your template, try to think of what elements will translate to another place in the process, thus contributing to implementing traceability. Table 3-1 presents my preferred and practical use case template, annotated with a description of what to put in each part and, in italics, where that part will be used later in the process.

Case Study

In this section, for simplicity and clarity, I will only show you a completed form of every artifact. You have to be aware that within the overall activity, the artifacts discussed are maintained in parallel, and while refining one artifact you are likely to unveil changes that need to be applied to the related artifacts. More specifically, you are likely to observe a high level of interaction during the development of the following artifacts (as presented by the dotted lines in the process diagram of Figure 1-7 in Chapter 1): the use cases, the use case model with the actor model, and the user experience model.

System Vision and Features

The vision document for the case study can be found in Appendix B, "Books REasy Vision." I invite you to read it before proceeding with the rest of the discussion in this chapter.

The important aspect of the vision document is that it specifies the overall scope of the solution. Obviously, it is impossible to precisely define the scope at this level of abstraction. But the fact that there are enough elements to define some scope is one of the expected characteristics of a vision document. The subsequent work of system specification will further refine the scope.

Table 3-1: Annotated use case template.

Name	Name of the use case *(for identification)*.
Brief Description	A brief description that covers the goal of the system usage *(a use case exists to accomplish a goal of an Actor using the system; useful for consistency check for the use case model)*.
Actor(s)	This is the Actor that initiates the system usage. If more than one Actor is listed, also present the abstract Actor that factors the commonality of the actual Actors within the context of this (and possibly other) use case(s). This helps in normalizing the Actor diagram, as explained later *(useful for consistency check for the use case model)*. For example, *Abstract Actor* A: Concrete Actor X, Concrete Actor Y, …

Flow of Events

Basic Flow

Define the sequence of actions that happen if everything goes well; what is expected to happen in a good day *(defines the main scenario in the sequence diagrams)*.

Alternate Flows

Title	**Description**
A brief identification	Describe one possible exceptional situation and the sequence of actions that happen *(defines exceptional scenarios in the sequence diagrams)*. *(Repeat rows as needed)*.

Pre-Conditions

Title	**Description**
A brief identification	Describe what needs to have happened in order for the Actor to be able to access the usage described *(useful in test cases for defining the initial state of the system before the test case starts)*. *(Repeat rows as needed)*.

Post-Conditions

Title	**Description**
A brief identification	Describe, in terms of goals achieved or missed, what is the situation after each possible flow of events *(useful in test cases for defining the expected final state of the system after the test case finishes)*. *(Repeat rows as needed)*.

Extension Points

What other use cases can optionally be triggered from this one *(defines the <extend> relationships in the use case model)*.

User Stories

As stated in the Approach, user stories are nonformal descriptions, written by the users, of what they expect that the system should do. Create a consensus on a list of sections that users need to write, which represent their understanding of possible system usage. Each user story can be seen as a detailed feature or functional requirement of the system. Allocate one or more sections to each user representative.

The identified sections are likely to represent use cases. Ask users to describe what the system does along with a description of who uses the system in the context of the described usage. Use the standard wording of "Description of the featured user" and "Description of what happens" in order to focus the thinking of the users writing these descriptions. Table 3-2 is an example of a user story describing the Registration. Note that you should use the table format for your own convenience; users should not use it, to keep them from trying to create too much structure.

The user story described in Table 3-2 is an example of what you are likely to get from the user representatives. Here are some interesting remarks that apply to this description:

- The text is free format and does not really help the use case analysis, which is an activity that takes place when creating the analysis model. Specifically, some parts of the text are expressed in the passive voice, which is the usual way to express requirements. Use cases describe usage and should be stated in the active voice. In the next activity, which is to define the use cases, we will rephrase these descriptions in a more appropriate format.

- You can find within the text the attributes of the business entities. The information for the attributes should be part of the glossary and need not (and should not) be repeated in a use case definition.

- The description lacks details and completeness:
  - It is reasonable to expect that when the users have successfully registered, they should also be signed-in when the interaction is completed.
  - The e-mail address should reject e-mail addresses that are not well-formed.

❑ The business rule about not allowing offending words is not referenced. The username, password, and e-mail should be validated for offending words.

The complete list of user stories can be found in Appendix C.

Table 3-2: Registration user story.

System Usage	Create Account

Description of the Featured User

The User is any individual who has accessed the BooksREasy Web site, and does not have an account on the system. A User like this can browse the catalogue and select books to order (but cannot place orders). The unregistered individual wants to register because they want to be able to place orders or because when they tried to place their first order they were prompted to register.

Description of What Happens

The User navigates to the BooksREasy Web site. The site should have a feature that indicates to the User that it supports registration. The User selects that feature, and the system should present the User with a Registration form where they must enter the following information:

■ Username
■ Password
■ E-mail address
■ Credit card information:
  ❑ Name on credit card
  ❑ Card number
  ❑ Card type
  ❑ Card expiration date
■ Billing address information:
  ❑ Street address
  ❑ City
  ❑ State
  ❑ ZIP/Postal Code
  ❑ Country

The User validates the input, and the system has to create the account. Situations where the system should reject the account creation are

■ The username already exists in the system.
■ The credit card is not valid.
■ Some item of information is missing.

Actors

Before we can proceed with the use case model, we first have to make an exhaustive list of the actors interacting with the system. Review the user stories and consolidate the descriptions and information describing the featured users. Then you can create an initial UML model of the actors. Note that this model is likely to evolve after you start writing the detailed definitions of the use cases.

Figure 3-1 shows the initial actor diagram, based on the user stories documented in Appendix C.

First, you have to note the existence of an actor named Anonymous User. You may find it unusual to represent an unregistered user, but if you think deeper you will see that it is, in fact, quite natural. Put yourself in the mindset of viewing the actors as roles. The user stories describe how nonauthenticated individuals can use the features of the site (as they do for all the other types of individuals).

We then can see these individuals on a par with the other actors and define what they can and cannot do within the site (as we do for all the other actors). In particular, we see that Registered Buyers and Admins, who are both authenticated types of users, have different rights when using the various features of the system. In Chapter 8 you will see that "actors" translate into "roles" in the role-based security framework of .NET. Role-based security is about securing the access to .NET elements of code which, in some way (at the corresponding level of abstraction), represent system functions. So there is a direct match in role-based security between the way actors use the system (functions) and roles.

Continuing our review of the initial actor model, we can easily see that it is not satisfactory in that it fails to represent a certain number of relationships. Indeed, it is clear from the user stories that both the Anonymous User actor and the Registered Buyer actor share some common capabilities. Specifically,

Figure 3-1: Initial UML diagram of actors.

both can search and browse the catalogue, add book items in a shopping cart, and update the shopping cart. Their main difference is that only the Registered Buyer can place orders. If we represent this common capability as another type of actor, Buyer, we can say that Anonymous User and Registered Buyer are a kind of Buyer, or specializations of Buyer. In Figure 3-2 you can see the representation of this situation in the actor model.

This approach of extracting commonalities and generalizing concepts can be seen as some kind of normalization of the model, in the same way that you are used to producing a normalized form of an entity-relationship model in database design. This normalization will be done at the same time that use cases are defined, when deciding which actors exercise each use case. See the discussion on abstract actors below.

Applying the same kind of reasoning between Registered Buyer and Admin, we see that the common capability in this case is to be registered on the system. We thus create a generalized role of Registered User and we end up with a new model as in Figure 3-3.

An important note is that both new generalized actors, Buyer and Registered User, are abstract. What this tells us is

- When writing use cases, you are allowed to specify an abstract actor as the actor exercising the use case. This is an important point, as it gives you a powerful technique for consistency check. Ideally, if a use case defines

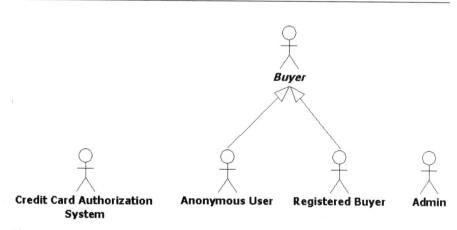

Figure 3-2: Anonymous User and Registered Buyer are a kind of Buyer.

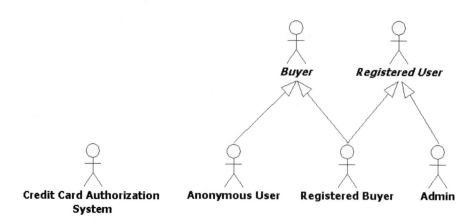

Figure 3-3: Admin and Registered Buyer are a kind of Registered User.

more than one concrete actor, it should also list one abstract actor (only one) that factors the commonality in behavior of these actors. The approach is based on the following axiom: If two actors exercise the same use case, then they have some commonality in their behavior and we can factor this commonality in an abstract actor (thus normalizing the actor model). After generalizing the behavior of actors into an abstract actor for the specific situation of two or more actors exercising a use case, we can replace the multitude of actors in the use case definition by one abstract actor. But for the sake of clarity in the documentation, it is better to just add it alongside the concrete actors. This approach in turn supports the technique of deriving the role-based security configuration from the actor model. If you can achieve this, you are also in good shape to have the right granularity for the use case. If, for example, you write a use case and find that two actors exercise the use case (e.g., Registered Buyer and Anonymous User), the reality is that Buyer exercises the use case. But thanks to the actor model, you know that you will be using the nonabstract roles of Registered Buyer and Anonymous User for the implementation. By the same token, trying to achieve only one actor per use case will help you unveil the commonalities between actors and thus help you create a good, normalized actor model. It is important to note that this approach implies a back-and-forth review of the actor model in relation with the use case definitions.

- Abstract actors will not correspond to any role in .NET role-based security. Only nonabstract (concrete) actors will turn into roles, and when a new user is created in the system, they should be allocated to one or more of these roles. This is also an important point to understand, that every actual system user can play more than one role, so they can be more than one actor. The question that you will have to answer when configuring the role-based security is, Do you want to allow a real user to be in two roles at the same time (access the union of the features of the two roles) or do you want to oblige a real user to assume a specific role upon authentication? In this case study I have chosen to allow an actual user to be only one actor (be in one role) at any time. But bear in mind that this question has only to do with the design mechanism, as presented in Chapter 6, and does not impact the use case model.

The model in Figure 3-3 actually tells us even more about what actors can and cannot do with the system—what usage is and is not allowed for each one. From the model, we can see directly that the actor Admin cannot be a Buyer, as it does not belong to any specialization path from Buyer. That means that Admins should not have access to any feature defined for Buyers (browsing catalogue, updating cart, checking out).

Later, when detailing the use cases, we will make the assumption that Admins can also access buying features. For this we just need to make the Admin a specialization of a Registered Buyer. This may look like a contrived example, but it will serve very well the purpose of demonstrating specialization within nonabstract actors as well as with the discussion of role-based security in Chapter 8. Figure 3-4 shows what happens to the actor model in this situation.

Use Case Model

As mentioned in the Approach, after producing the user stories, you have to identify an initial set of use cases. Let's review the information we have at this stage that will help us create this initial list:

- The user stories can be used directly to define candidate use cases.

- We also have defined the business use case model and the business object model. Of particular interest are the business workers of the business object model. You can start by defining a candidate system actor for each business worker, unless the business worker is to be automated. Then, define a candidate use case for every responsibility of each business worker in each business use case.

- Finally, you can use the vision document, particularly the functional features section for a consistency check.

Based on the user stories, we have the following candidate use cases: Create Account, Manage Account, Sign-In, Sign-Out, Browse Store Catalogue, Review Shopping Cart, Check-Out, Manage Users.

By examining the business models, we can identify the business workers: Customer Management, Credit Card Handling, and Store. The Customer Management and Store are business workers that correspond precisely to what

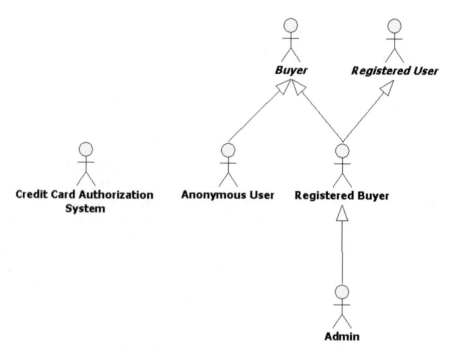

Figure 3-4: Admin is a kind of Registered Buyer.

our solution will automate, so there is no need to create system actors for them. We also make the assumption that Credit Card Handling will be supported by an external system, thus we will not automate this business worker as part of our solution (it has already been automated). As a consequence, because it will not be automated by our system, Credit Card Handling should be represented as a system actor, namely Credit Card Authorization System (as represented in the Actor model).

The fact that it is already automated does not have any impact on the system design. We will see later in Chapters 5 and 6 that its interaction with the system will follow the same pattern as for any other system actor, in the sense that the interaction will happen through boundary classes. The only specificity is that we will name these boundary classes "adapters," in order to stay consistent with the common terminology in the industry. An adapter defines the interface we need to have to an external system, and thus the perspective our system has of the external system. The usage of adapters also has important implications for security, as they will help to integrate the external system into the overall role-based security configuration, which we will discuss in Chapter 8.

Considering now the combination of business use cases and business workers, we have the following candidate use cases: Customer Management—Register, Customer Management—Manage Account, Credit Card Handling—Register, and Credit Card Handling—Manage Account. To keep the discussion to the point and because the focus is on the refinement of the registration function, I will not consider the rest of the business use cases, which fall in the Store organizational unit. The use cases defined in that unit are Browse Book Catalogue and Place Order; the business workers involved are Customer Management, Credit Card Handling, and Store.

Considering the Customer Management organizational unit, the candidate system use cases Customer Management—Register and Customer Management—Manage Account have already been identified as Create Account and Manage Account. The other two use cases, Credit Card Handling—Register and Credit Card Handling—Manage Account come from the business worker Credit Card Handling. Although we could represent them in the initial use case model, the fact is that the usage covered by these use cases is already described within the corresponding Create Account and Manage Account use cases. Thus, we might as well integrate them directly in the corresponding ones. Notice also that the business model alone did not lead to the identification of the two use cases, Sign-In and Sign-Out, which are also parts of the Customer Management functionality.

Putting all this together, you can see in Figures 3-5 through 3-7 the UML diagrams representing the identified use case and system actors with their relationships.

Scope Map

Reviewing Figures 3-5 through 3-7, we notice that they define some kind of organization for the identified use cases. In Figure 3-5 we have represented the following use cases: Create Account, Manage Account, Sign-In, and Sign-Out. Figure 3-6 shows these use cases: Browse Store Catalogue, Review Shopping Cart, Check-Out, and Sign-In. Note that the Sign-In use case is mainly there for the purpose of showing the extend relationship it has with Check-Out (see the use case template presented earlier for a description of the extend relationship). What we see is a separation of concerns that can be expressed as follows: Figure 3-5 presents the use cases related to User Account Manage-

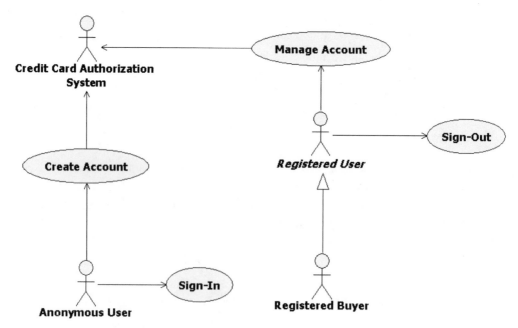

Figure 3-5: Use case model: User Account Management.

ment, Figure 3-6 presents the use cases related to Store Front, and Figure 3-7 presents the use cases related to Maintenance.

It is a good practice to group the related use cases together into use case packages. In our case study we have three packages: User Account Management, Store Front, and Maintenance. Though we have only one level of hierarchy, for more complex and extensive systems you might well need to group sets of use case packages into a higher-level package, a lower-level package, and so on.

This organization can also be graphically represented in a variety of ways. A very simple way to represent these hierarchies is a tree structure as depicted

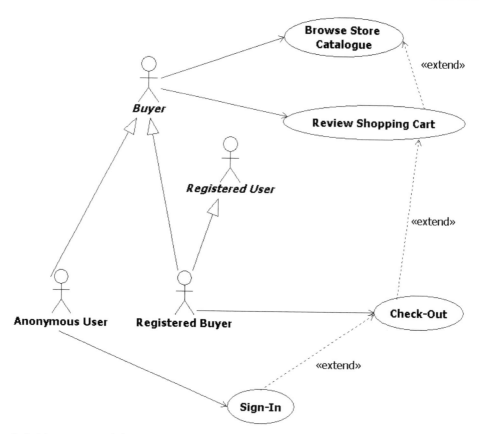

Figure 3-6: Use case model: Store Front.

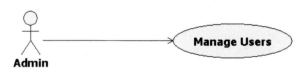

Figure 3-7: Use case model: Maintenance.

in Figure 3-8. It is very common for software tools to represent hierarchies this way, and you are likely to find them in most of the UML modeling tools.

The advantage of organizing use cases into packages is that you effectively structure the scope of the system. Indeed, as presented earlier, a use case is the ultimate level of detailing the system's features, hence the scope of the system. Applying structure to the scope enables you to better comprehend the complexity of the system. This in turn helps you make the right decisions as to which part is the most important and should be given priority, and ultimately it gives you an effective tool to define development iterations. You now have the answer to the big questions: What should I put in a specific iteration? How many iterations do I need?

For our case study, we shall give priority to the User Account Management package; therefore, we will develop it in the first iteration. This choice is quite sensible, as authenticating users is the first thing that needs to happen in order

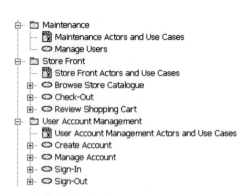

Figure 3-8: Use cases organized in a tree structure.

to authorize them to access all the other features the system will eventually propose, represented by the other use case packages.

I would also like to mention that a mind map is another way to represent scope and hierarchies in general. This is a very powerful tool to organize knowledge and can very well be used to structure the use cases, also. The advantage of using a mind-map tool is that during the system specification activities you will be talking to a lot of nontechnical users. These users are more likely to have been using a mind-map tool in their day-to-day job, rather than a UML modeling tool.

Using a mind-map tool can also be beneficial in the vision document. Instead of defining a list of features, you can have a mind map of all features, functional or not, and organize them in clusters: first separating functional from nonfunctional, then subdividing the functional into smaller clusters down to the level of detail you expect to see in a vision document. Using this technique during inception (i.e., producing the vision document) can also help the various stakeholders to better comprehend the scope of the system at a higher level than use cases. From there, it might well be decided to chunk the development of the system into wider phases, each phase defining a project of its own, with its own iterations.

Finally, some mind-mapping tools have extensibility interfaces and can be integrated with other tools. Thus, the mind map you have defined for the functional requirements in the vision document can be used to generate the initial structure of use case packages in the UML modeling tool. Conversely, you can produce a mind-map format report out of the use case package structure defined in your UML modeling tool. Figure 3-9 shows a mind-map example of representing the use cases and their package organization.

Figure 3-9: Use cases organized in a mind map.

Use Cases

Having established which of the use cases are to be developed in the first iteration, you will need to describe them in every possible detail. Defining use cases is the most critical activity of this use case-driven process. As such, it is important to develop the right skills in writing use cases, and I will show you a certain number of critical elements that you should pay attention to in doing so. But this particular topic is so vast, it would take the rest of the book to describe it. Fortunately, there are some very good books out there to help you complete your knowledge, like the very detailed *Object-Oriented Software Engineering: A Use Case Driven Approach* and *Use Case Modeling* or the very practical *Applying Use Case Driven Object Modeling with UML: An Annotated e-Commerce Example* (where you can find checklists of the most common mistakes to avoid and also of the most effective things to do).

Here is a quick list of the most important elements to keep in mind while writing use cases:

- In writing the text, strive to use the format noun-verb-noun throughout. Make sure that the business entities stand out in the text. At the same time avoid creating a pedantic description, as the use cases are aimed at users, and the flow of the text should be natural. Give some consideration to the thought that the use case texts can be used as the basis of the user's manual (see *Use Case Driven Object Modeling with UML: A Practical Approach*).

- Use cases describe the system usage by the user. You therefore need to take the perspective of the user, writing in active voice and using present tense.

- Use only words found in the business and system glossaries. If a new word needs to be used, define it in one of them.

- Do not reference class methods or operations in the use case text, because they describe *How* the system will do things as opposed to *What* the system will do, which is the concern of the use cases.

- Ask yourself if you really describe *What* the system does and not *How* it does it.

- Make sure all the business rules appear in some use cases. Use the business rules as hints for alternate paths.

Applying the preceding discussion to the Create Account use case, we obtain the detailed description shown in Table 3-3. For completeness, Appendix D lists the User Account Management use cases depicted in the use case diagram of Figure 3-5.

From the use case description in Table 3-3 you notice that when exercising this use case, upon completion, the user assumes the role of Registered Buyer. To assume a role of Admin, we would need to have another use case, possibly complementary to this one with another actor (e.g., Site Administrator) who does not inherit from any other actor. Because an Admin is a kind of Registered Buyer, we could have a use case named "Upgrade User to Administrator." I have chosen not to consider this use case, mainly because of the inherently contrived nature of the relationship between Admin and Registered Buyer, but also because it will not add much value to the discussion (while bringing unnecessary complexity to the case study).

If you are still unsure about your use cases being complete and unambiguous, there is an optional extra step that you can take as a consistency check. Create some sequence diagrams of the use cases as depicted in Figure 3-10 for basic flow of events of the Create Account use case. The visual representation of the flow of information can often be of great help while writing the description of the use cases.

To create this diagram, take each step of the basic flow and represent it in the left of the diagram. Then represent the system actors and the system as lifelines. Do not represent anything else; remember that you are talking to the user representatives and they are not supposed to understand objects and methods. Represent as a message the flow of information taking place at each step of the flow of events.

Table 3-3: Detailed description for Create Account use case.

Name	Create Account
Brief Description	The Create Account use case allows the User to create and activate an account, which contains information about the User.
	Upon successful account creation, the User is also signed in.
	The User is created with a role of Registered Buyer.
Actor(s)	Anonymous User.

Flow of Events

Basic Flow

This use case starts when the User accesses the Create Account feature of the system.

1. The system displays the *User Account* information that needs to be entered for the User.

2. The User enters the required *User Account* information values and requests that the system save the entered values. The system validates the User Account data entered by the user.

3. The system also validates the *Credit Card* by submitting a *Credit Card* validation request to the Credit Card Authorization System.

4. The system then displays the entered data and asks the User to confirm that an account should be created with the entered values.

5. The User confirms that an account should be created. A new account is created and activated for the User. The *User Account* data provided is stored in the User's new account. The system also assigns the User to the group of Registered Buyers and stores this information in relation to the User Account.

6. The system signs in the User under the newly created account. The system notifies the User that the account has been activated and that the new values have been saved.

7. The use case ends.

Alternate Flows

User Cancels Request	At any time, the User may choose to cancel the current operation. If the User cancels during account creation, the account is not created.
User Enters Invalid User Account Information	If the system determines that the User entered invalid *User Account* information the following occurs:

- The system describes what data was invalid and presents the User with suggestions for entering valid data.
- The system prompts the User to re-enter the *User Account* information.
- The User re-enters the information and the system revalidates it.
- If valid information is entered, the *User Account* information is stored.
- If invalid data is entered, the "User Enters Invalid User Account Information" alternative flow is executed again. This repeats until valid information is entered or until the User cancels the Create Account request.

Invalid *User Account* information:

- Missing information items.
- Username already exists in the system.
- *User Account* information entered does not comply with its definition in the glossary.
- Not well-formed e-mail address.
- *Credit Card* is not valid.
- Offending words in any part of the *User Account* information.

Pre-Conditions

Title	Description
None	

Post-Conditions

Title	Description
Success	The User Account was created and activated and the User is signed in as a role of Registered Buyer.
The User Account Was Not Created	This occurs when the User fails to enter valid *User Account* data or if the User chooses to cancel the Create Account request. In such a case, the account is not created.

Extension Points

None

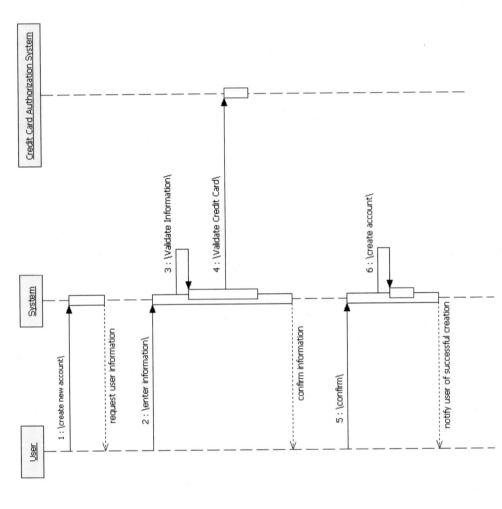

This use case starts when the User indicates to the system that he/she wishes to create an account.

The system displays the User Information that needs to be entered for the User.

The User enters the required User Information values and requests that the system save the entered values.

The system validates the entered User Information.

The system also validates the Credit Card by submitting a Credit Card validation request to the Credit Card Authorization System.

The system then displays the entered information and asks the User to confirm that an account should be created with the entered values.

The User confirms that an account should be created.

A new account is created and activated for the User. The entered User Information is stored in the User's new account.

The system signs in the User under the newly created account. The system notifies the User that his/her account has been activated and that the new values have been saved.

Figure 3-10: Sequence diagram of Create Account use case.

Summary

In this chapter we reviewed the activities related to system requirements capture. With these activities you produce five artifacts: vision document, user stories, use cases, use case model (including the actor diagram), and system glossary. You also organize use cases into a hierarchy of packages and use this hierarchy as a scope map to prioritize the work by assigning packages to software development iterations. An important note is that the use cases need to be checked for consistency with the user experience model, which we will review in Chapter 4.

The vision document specifies the overall scope of the solution and puts it in context with the business needs of the various stakeholders. In this document, you will find the problem definition, the stakeholders and their concerns and responsibilities, the high-level features, and any other type of high-level constraint of the solution.

The user stories are an intermediate step, which is very helpful in situations where the users are not experienced in working with use cases.

User stories are useful to produce the initial set of use cases and the corresponding use case model. Particular attention has to be paid to the model of the actors, which has to be normalized by extracting common capabilities of the system actors. When you organize the use cases into a hierarchy of packages, you effectively have a scope map. You use the scope map to visualize the extent of the system, prioritize the use cases, and define software development iterations.

Use case definitions are the core of the system specification. They describe the required behavior in great detail, with precision, and without any ambiguity. By taking the user perspective when describing use cases, you can describe *What* the system does and avoid describing *How* it operates. How the system operates is a concern of the system design, not the system specification. Write the use cases from the perspective of the user, using active voice and present tense. Try to write text that is close to a noun-verb-noun format, where each noun has to exist in the glossaries.

During requirements definition, you will also maintain the business glossary and define the system glossary, with the terms that are specific to the system development.

The information captured in the use case model and the user experience model will later be integrated to create the analysis model in system design.

Chapter 4

User Experience Model

Introduction

We first need to define the user experience model. It is a visual specification of the user interface of the system. This specification covers the user interface elements and their navigation. The concern of user experience modeling is purely related to representing the system data to the user and does not cover the study of attractiveness or visual appeal of the user interface. These considerations are specifically important when developing a commerce Web site for the public (business to consumer) and should be addressed as another aspect of specification, beyond the UML modeling of the user interface. The process presented in this book does not cover these issues. This chapter is a concise but complete presentation of the user experience modeling concepts and activities as described in RUP; they are further described in *Building Web Applications with UML (Second Edition)*.

In the introduction of the process in Chapter 1, as well as in Chapter 3, I have mentioned the development of the user experience model in parallel with the development of the use cases and the use case model. This is represented in Figure 1-7 (in Chapter 1) by the dotted lines going in both directions between the use case model and the user experience model. You could think that this approach may foster the definitions of bad use cases, because the users will think more in terms of how the system will do things in place of what it will do for the user. This is indeed a risk, which you can alleviate by applying the basic principles for writing good use cases presented in Chapter 3. On the other hand, there are considerable advantages to using this approach.

For one, a user experience model does not really express how the system will do things, but what the system will look like from the perspective of the user. In use cases we often find the phrase construct "The system displays ..." This construct conveys a semantic of presenting a form to the user. Again, if you recall how you were thinking when doing business modeling, the correct mindset is to take the perspective of an exchange of paper forms between the system and the user. After all, the system is just the automation of one or more business workers who would otherwise physically handle the forms. In this context, the user experience model is a direct transformation of the words in the use cases into representations of screens. The correct mindset for this activity is to ask how the user will be carrying the task defined by the use case, effectively capturing the mental task model of the user. This is different from how the system will do the work.

Here also lies the second advantage of developing the user experience model along with the use case model, which is the integration of the user's pictorial thinking. Every individual uses different ways of thinking: words, but also pictures and numbers. It is commonly admitted that most people primarily think in terms of pictures (hence the saying, "A picture is worth a thousand words"). By representing user interaction in diagrams, the users find a helpful tool to check the consistency of the use case descriptions.

Finally, we have to consider that both models involve the contribution of the user representatives, which is an indication of the level of interaction and interdependency between these two models. As both models are sourcing from the user community, they both contribute to the overall definition of the specification of the system. The use case model represents what services the system will give to the user, and the user experience model represents the mental task model of the user.

Approach

As presented in Chapters 1 and 3, user stories are the starting point for developing the user experience model; they give you a strong sense of what functionality the system will support. From these you can produce the initial use case model, which is important to identify the actors and have a visual representation of the system functions. Then you can use the initial use case model along with the user stories to get an initial draft of the user experience model. After this you should refine both the use case model and the user experience model in parallel, as presented in the Introduction, which explains the rationale of this approach.

The user experience model is divided into two parts, representing the static and dynamic aspects of the system. In both these dimensions, it is advisable to organize the representations into packages that follow the same structure defined in the use case model, as depicted in Figure 4-1 (in this figure, and subsequently in this book, you will find the abbreviation "Ux" for "user experience").

User Experience Model Elements

The static aspect is captured in the user experience model elements and the associated navigation maps. It is important to understand that the user experi-

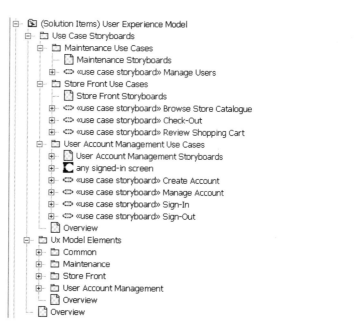

Figure 4-1: User experience model structure.

ence model deals exclusively with the concept of the screen. The part of the model describing the model elements defines the list of screens that make up the user interface. Screens are related to each other with associations, which identify expected navigational pathways; thus, the navigation maps convey the structure of the user experience model. Screens are represented as classes with the stereotype of "screen."

Some screens contain input forms that represent sets of input fields used to receive user information. You can identify input forms in use cases by looking for descriptions where the system requires the user to enter data representing a business entity (e.g., in the Create Account use case, "The system displays the *User Information* that needs to be entered for the User").

Input forms are represented as classes with a stereotype of "input form." In the example above, the business entity is *User Information* and the corresponding input form will contain input fields that correspond to the list of attributes of that object, as defined in the glossary. Input forms can be used with different screens, which aggregate input forms. Figure 4-2 presents an example of the aggregation relationship between two screens and an input form. Note that the relationship is a composition, as the screen owns the input form. If the input form needs to be prepopulated with default values (as is the case for the Account Info Form when used by the Manage Account screen), you need to add in the screen class one attribute for each corresponding attribute in the input form that needs to be prepopulated.

Defining an initial list of screens is the first step, and this can be achieved by examining the user stories (and subsequently the use cases). As pointed out in the Introduction, if you take the mindset of considering the user interaction as an exchange of a series of forms between the user and the system, it is very likely that you will be able to identify the bulk of the screens that you need to describe the interaction. For each screen you should define the following elements:

- The user actions that should be available to the user. These represent the features of the system that are accessible to a specific role at a specific time, defined by the context of the use case. A good practice is to use the word "feature" in the use case descriptions, as demonstrated with the BooksREasy use cases. The user actions are modeled as operations (e.g., in Figure 4-2 we define the "modify password" operation on the Manage Account screen).

- The environment actions on the screen. These are the actions that the environment (the Web browser or the Web server) performs on the

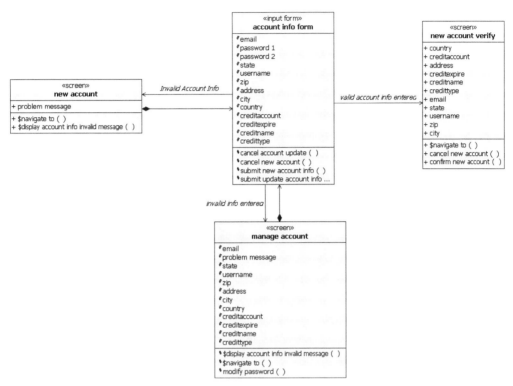

Figure 4-2: Screen and input form relationship.

screen. Typically that would be creation, redirection, and display actions. At this level of analysis it is not appropriate to represent any details of the technical architecture. However, it is useful to model these actions, as they help in creating the storyboards and thus getting a better understanding of the dynamics of the user interface. The convention is to model these actions as operations with their name beginning with a "$". Intuitively you should add an action of "$navigate to" for each screen.

- One environment action for each message that can be displayed on the screen. This is a useful approach that fosters completeness of the specifications, as these messages are rarely captured in any other part of the model. They are also helpful for creating semantically richer storyboards. These are usually messages of information, which the system sends to the user to notify them of the state of the system. It can be an error message or an information message about the completion of the use case. An example would be a message to inform the user that the account creation was successful, at the same time that the system presents the home account page when the user is logged in. Note that this discussion does not cover the static screen elements as text, titles, images, and field labels, as these elements do not need to be modeled. The convention for modeling the screen messages is to define two elements:

□ An attribute in the screen class, which represents the real estate that the message will take up on the screen. The name of this attribute should represent a message type (conceptually mapped to a region of the page), and not the actual message, which is supposed to be dynamic. In Figure 4-2 the attribute "problem message" in the Manage Account class represents a message that will explain to the user why the data entered is invalid. Intuitively we expect that the message will be different depending on what error(s) the user made.

□ One operation in the class for each message that needs to be displayed. These operations are named according to the specific message to display; the convention is to also begin their name with a "$". In Figure 4-2 the operation "$display account info invalid message" of the Manage Account class models the display of the corresponding message.

■ The dynamic content of the screen. This is the content that the system will have to provide as part of how it implements the use case. It covers mainly the business information managed by the system. You can identify the content by reviewing the use cases for terms appearing in the business or system glossary, in a phrase of the type "the system displays <business or system glossary term>". This phrase construct helps you differentiate dynamic content from input forms, where the user has to enter information. By reviewing the definition of the term you can define what has to appear on the screen. The dynamic content is modeled as attributes; for example, in Figure 4-2 the New Account Verify screen displays for confirmation all the user account attributes, as they have been captured by the system. On this screen the fields are not input fields.

Screen Mock-ups

Another important type of user experience artifact to consider is the screen mock-up. This artifact does not fall directly in the realm of user experience modeling but has to be considered as part of the system specification. Optionally, you can link a screen with a screen mock-up, presented in the form of a bitmap or pure HTML document (or any other way you deem appropriate and practical in the context of your project).

Navigation Maps

The navigation map represents the expected navigational pathways between screens. Create one map for each package of related use cases. In the navigation map, you represent only the screens and input forms with their names and associations, excluding any details of attributes and operations. The navigation map is meant to be a summary of the structure of the user interface. The details of the screens will appear in the participants diagram for each storyboard, which focuses on one single use case and thus involves only a subset of the screens presented in the navigation maps. To represent the navigational paths, you relate the screens with directed association relationships as depicted in Figure 4-3.

Some notes on modeling the navigation paths:

- Unless obvious, it is a good practice to identify each association with a name that represents the action that has initiated the navigation.

- Because a single screen can contain multiple forms, and because each form can have its own actions attached, you should link the navigation associations to the input forms and not to their parent screen (e.g., in Figure 4-3, there is an association from "account info form" to "new account verify" because the navigation is initiated by the action of submitting the input form.

- You should not consider any navigation from a screen to any of its input forms, as the input forms are rendered at the same time with the parent screen.

The navigation map does not represent all the possible navigations between the screens but only the ones captured in the use cases. This is an important point to understand: The user experience model does not represent more information than defined in the use cases, and the navigational paths should be analyzed only in relation to the use case descriptions. You should be able to trace every navigational path to a flow of events in a use case.

To address usability and control the complexity of the user task, try to keep every screen within three navigational steps of the home screen. This is also a good consistency check for the structure of the use cases, as a complex navigation path denotes a complex structure of the underlying task represented by

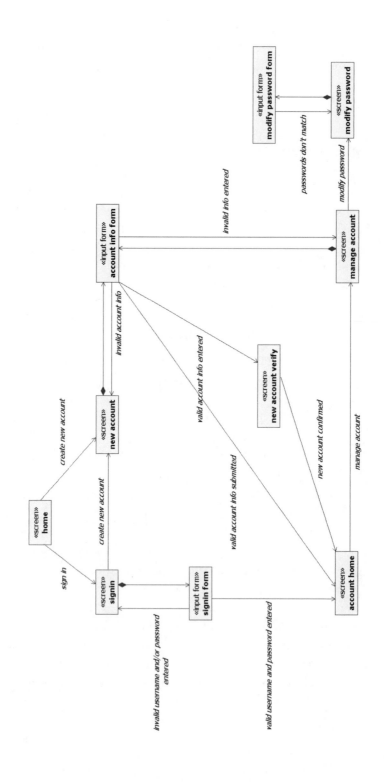

Figure 4-3: User Account Management navigation map.

the use case. If a situation like this occurs, you should carefully review the corresponding use cases with the users. Although it is notorious that most people will skip doing manual consistency checks, remember that software engineering imposes a disciplined approach to the way you work.

Use Case Storyboards

The dynamic aspect of the user experience model is represented with the use case storyboards. You define a use case storyboard for each use case that has a graphical user interaction, modeled by a realization relationship between the storyboard and the corresponding use case, thus effectively implementing traceability for this artifact. This is depicted in Figure 4-4 for the User Account Management use cases.

Storyboards are the transpositions, in terms of screen collaborations, of one specific instance of the flow of events of a use case. For each storyboard you define two types of diagrams—a flow diagram and a participants diagram.

The flow diagram, depicted in Figure 4-5, is a sequence diagram representing the collaboration of the user and the screens involved in the realization of the task represented by the use case. There is one flow diagram for each possible flow of events identified in the corresponding use case, and you

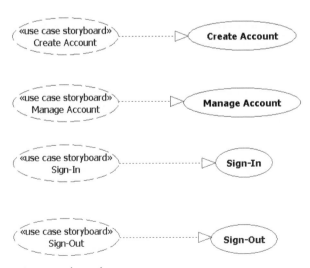

Figure 4-4: Tracing storyboards to use cases.

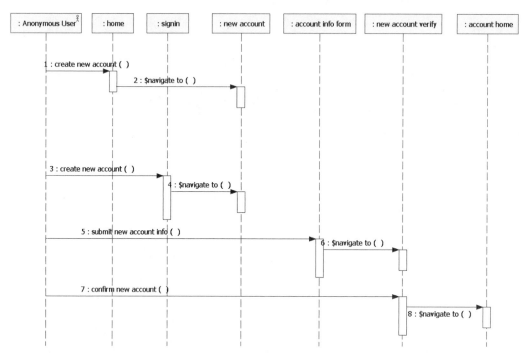

Figure 4-5: Flow diagram: Basic flow of Create Account use case.

should create at least the flow diagram corresponding to the basic flow of events of each use case. The messages that you find on a flow diagram must match the operations defined in the corresponding classes. As you will see later in Chapter 5, sequence diagrams are the central element of the process because they capture the dynamics of the system. They are the central point where all consistency checks and validations of other models take place. This is no different with the flow diagrams, and you should use them to validate both the navigation maps and the flow of events of the use cases.

A participants diagram, depicted in Figure 4-6, is a subset of a navigation map, which contains the screens and input forms involved in the user interaction for the specific use case. That means that you create one participants diagram per storyboard, thus covering all the flow diagrams for that storyboard. In this participants diagram you represent the screens and input forms with all their detail, thus effectively complementing the flow diagram where these elements are presented only with their names.

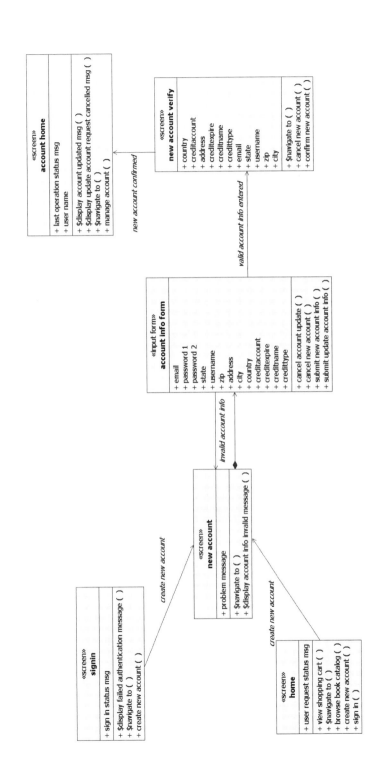

Figure 4-6: Participants diagram: Create account use case.

Case Study

Navigation Maps

Continuing the specification of the User Account Management function, and specifically the Create Account use case, we will examine the related user experience artifacts.

As presented in the Approach, we examine the user stories to identify an initial set of screens, input forms, and their navigations. We can identify the following user experience elements:

- "The user navigates to the BooksREasy Web site": We identify some sort of general "home" screen.

- "The site should have a feature which indicates to the user that it supports the registration": Reading the word "feature" we can identify that "home" needs to have an operation to provide for this user action, namely "create new account"; this operation defines a navigation from "home" to a second screen that will support the registration feature, "new account."

- "The user selects that feature, and the system should present the user with a registration form where the user must enter the following information": We identify that the site should have an input form for entering account information, "account info form," owned by "new account" screen. As expected, we need some validation user action, "submit new account info," which is represented by an operation in the input form. Similarly, we can expect to have a cancellation user action, "cancel new account."

- The list of information specified in the user story defines the attributes of "account info form."

- As there are some possible error situations described, we can also expect to have navigability from "account info form" to its parent "create new account" to capture the fact that the user will be advised of the error but still be presented with the "create new account" screen to correct it. The corresponding operation on the "create new account" screen is named "$display account info invalid message" and has an associated attribute, "problem message," as explained in the Approach.

All this is very straightforward, and we can create the initial navigation map, presented in Figure 4-7, which represents our current knowledge and understanding of the system, based on the Create Account user story.

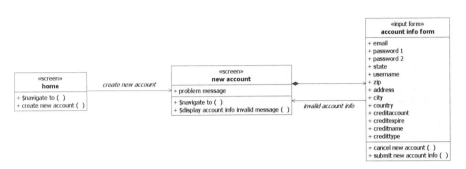

Figure 4-7: Initial navigation map: Create Account user story.

Although this looks like a good start, by examining the diagram we can directly spot at least one problem: What happens to the navigation when the data entered in the "account info form" is valid? There is nothing in the user story that gives a clue about answering this question. This is an example where the user experience model is useful in order to further refine the use cases, and you can now begin to understand the nature of the parallel development of the user experience model and the use cases.

When the Create Account use case is completed, we also uncover the existence of a "new account verify" screen and an "account home" screen, which answers the previous question.

You can review in Figure 4-3 the complete navigation map for the User Account Management use case package, which also covers the Create Account use case.

Use Case Storyboards

Having identified the user experience elements for one use case, you can proceed with developing the corresponding storyboard. As an initial step you should also use the user stories to create a complete and consistent set of artifacts. Notice that there are no alternate paths described in the user stories, thus the only flow diagram that we can initially create will be describing the user interaction for the basic flow of events.

As presented in the Approach, you create one storyboard per use case identified in the use case model, and as a consequence, the initial set of storyboards will match the set of user stories. But, looking back to Chapter 3, chances are that there will be a high level of consistency between the set of user stories and the set of use cases, so that you need to expect only a limited amount of rework. This rework should happen as soon as you have settled on the initial use case model and use case organization into packages. After this manual synchronization of this set of artifacts, you should keep the structures of both models consistent with each other. The other approach is to define the storyboards only after you have defined the initial use case model. Which approach you choose will largely depend on the team structure of your project.

Because we base the initial user experience model on the user stories, you can directly produce the participants diagram for one storyboard, while you analyze the user experience elements for the corresponding user story. In the participants diagram you represent the screens, the input forms with all their details, along with their navigation paths. Figure 4-7 showed an initial participants diagram for the Create Account user story; this diagram is also a part of the overall initial navigation map.

Figure 4-8 depicts the flow diagram representing the flow of events in the corresponding user story.

Being a sequence diagram, the flow diagram presents the dynamic behavior of the user interface. Because of this, Figure 4-8 makes even more

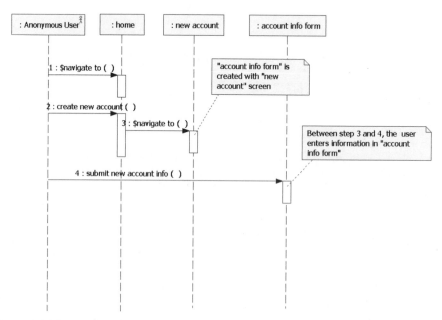

Figure 4-8: Initial flow diagram: Create Account user story.

apparent the missing navigation from the "account info form" mentioned earlier. Notice also that all messages in the diagram correspond to the actual operations defined in the user experience elements classes. It is important to consistently apply this approach in designing these diagrams, as it warrants the most accurate representation of the interaction and better helps to unveil possible shortcomings in the use case descriptions.

You can find in Figure 4-5 the complete flow diagram produced after detailing the Create Account use case, thus representing the end result of the activity. Also, in Figure 4-6 you can review the completed participants diagram for this use case.

Screen Mock-ups

Notwithstanding any possible screen where the user can initiate the Create Account use case, this use case involves two screens that we have chosen to mock-up in HTML. Figure 4-9 presents the Create Account page that depicts

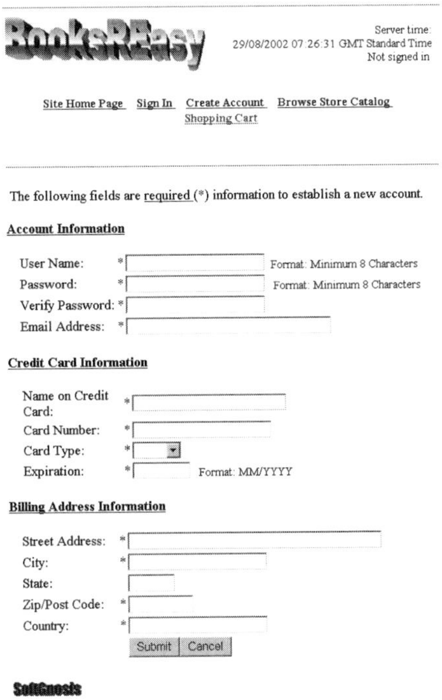

Figure 4-9: Create Account page.

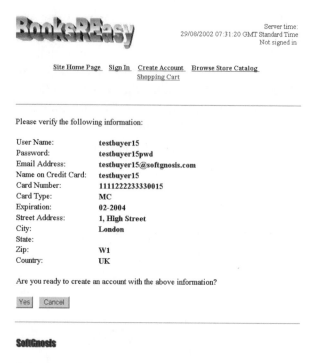

Figure 4-10: Verify Account page.

the "new account" screen with its "account info form" input form, while Figure 4-10 presents the Verify Account page that depicts the "new account verify" screen.

Using Microsoft Visual Studio .NET, it is very easy to create the design of Web forms and controls, the same way that you would create a user interface in an environment like Visual Basic. Creating the screen mock-ups with Microsoft Visual Studio .NET has the advantage of effectively creating at the same time the initial version of the Web forms and Web controls of the application.

Summary

In this chapter we reviewed the activities related to developing the user experience model, which is first developed from the user stories and later refined in parallel with the use cases, as it is very helpful to validate the flow of events of the use cases. The activities involved produce two artifacts—navigation maps and use case storyboards; storyboards consist of flow diagrams and a participants diagram. These models deal only with user interface elements: screens and input forms, both represented as classes in the UML models. These define the user experience model elements. Screens own input forms, and both contain attributes that represent dynamic content or messages, and operations that represent user or environment actions.

You create one navigation map per use case package, and one use case storyboard per use case. Within the storyboard you create one participants diagram and at least one flow diagram for the basic flow of events of the use case. Optionally, you create more flow diagrams for alternate flows of events.

The navigation map presents the user experience model elements with their associations, which represent the valid navigation paths between screens or input forms.

The use case storyboards represent the realization of the flow of events for the use cases that involves a graphical user interaction. Within a storyboard, the flow diagrams represent the sequence of screen navigations, which are needed to execute the user task defined in the flow of events of the corresponding use case. The participants diagram presents in detail the screens and input forms involved in all the flow diagrams of one storyboard, along with their navigation paths. As such it is a subset of a navigation map.

The user experience model is a transposition of the flow of events of a use case and does not contain more information. Thus, the navigational paths should be analyzed only in relation to the use case descriptions.

Part II

System Analysis and Design

Chapter 5

Analysis Model

Introduction

As introduced in Chapter 1, the analysis model is an intermediary step between system specification and detailed design, and helps you get a head start in the design, thus avoiding the analysis paralysis phenomenon. You will rarely find an advocate promoting the development and maintenance of the analysis model; most literature today proposes the development of an initial analysis model that will be gradually refined to become the design model. I encourage developing and maintaining an analysis model for two reasons:

- It is at this stage that most teams lose the plot of traceability. Indeed, it is a huge leap to go from use cases, use case models, and user experience models to design and implementation models, and if you do not represent in some form the process of crossing it, development people will find themselves disconnected from the functional specifications. They will not have a clear picture of where the things they develop come from and thus will not be able to effectively contribute in feeding back any problems they may come across.

■ I do promote the idea that the analysis model could be developed by functional analysts/architects, who are not supposed to deal with the technology and the code, but should understand UML. An important finality of the analysis model is also to validate the use cases, which implies the involvement of functional analysts/architects, as the keepers of the use cases. The analysis model has to be a high-level description of the design, avoiding technology, implementation, and code details. A functional analyst is better positioned to achieve this goal than a software architect (who might be tempted, because of their knowledge and skills, to define too many details)—unless the software architect is able to mentally switch their role to be a functional analyst/architect in the context of developing the analysis model.

Because of the relative high level of abstraction of the analysis model, the effort allocated to its development and maintenance can be kept to a fraction of the design effort (and an even smaller fraction of the overall system development effort). Because of this, it is highly desirable to follow this approach and systematically develop and maintain the analysis model. The payout in terms of the capability of tracing the artifacts is, in most cases, worth the extra effort.

Approach

At this stage of the process, we are working within one specific development iteration, and the subsequent activities will be focusing on the use cases that have been selected for implementation in this iteration. The input artifacts used for the analysis model are detailed use cases, use case model, user experience model, and the business entities model.

Model Structure

The overall structure of the model is very similar to the structure of the user experience model. You also break down the model between static and dynamic representations, as depicted in Figure 5-1. Each part is organized around the use case packages identified in the use case model.

Figure 5-1: Analysis model structure.

It is important to understand that while the objective of the analysis model is to realize the use cases, it should at the same time integrate the information gathered within the user experience model. This is represented in a simplified form in the overall process diagram in Figure 1-7 of Chapter 1, where there is one arrow sourcing from the use case model and another one sourcing from the user experience model, both flowing towards the analysis model. To represent this situation in UML, we define two relationships for each use case realization, as depicted in Figure 5-2. One relationship is the realization of the use case, and the other represents a trace dependency to represent that some model elements involved in the use case realization are traced back to the user experience model, in the context of the corresponding use case storyboard. At the same time, the diagram shows the realization dependency from the storyboard to the use case, as described in Chapter 4.

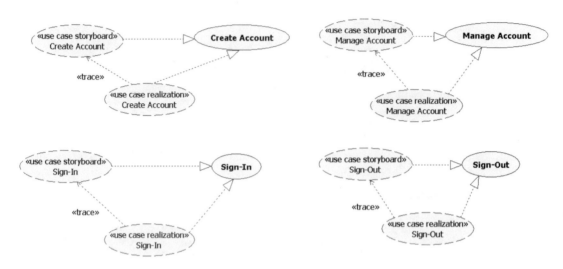

Figure 5-2: Tracing use case realizations to use cases and storyboards.

Key Abstractions—Managed Entities

At this point, it is important to understand that the analysis model deals with classes that represent the following generic concepts (depicted within a UML diagram in Figure 5-3, with their respective stereotype shapes):

- Boundary classes have two goals. They are primarily used to model the interaction of the system with the real world; in particular, they model the user interface. Ultimately in detailed design, they will turn into their counterparts of the underlying technology; for example, in .NET that will be Web forms (.aspx) and Web controls (.ascx), with their associated code-

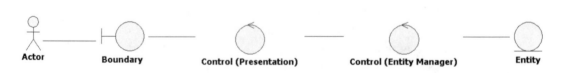

Figure 5-3: Boundary, control, and entity classes.

behind classes (.aspx.cs, ascx.cs). As you would expect, actors can only communicate with boundary classes. Boundary classes, in turn, can communicate with actors, other boundary classes, and control classes, mainly presentation-type control classes. The second goal of the boundary classes is to model the interaction with external systems (represented as actors), in which case they do not represent any user interface element and they are referred to as adapters. These classes will turn into simple .NET classes (.cs).

■ Control classes hold the behavioral logic of the system, by capturing the control logic of one or a few use cases. They can represent either business logic or presentation logic. Presentation logic control classes are destined to implement the sequence of events in the use case realization. Business logic control classes are the so-called entity managers, which are classes that control the access to one or more related entity classes, thus defining a business interface to these classes (this approach is similar to the one consisting of defining type models in *Objects, Components, and Frameworks with UML: The Catalysis Approach*). The control class is the coordinator of the activities of other classes, within a specific system function. Control classes can communicate with any type of class, except the actors. Control classes will turn into code (.cs in .NET). A careful design of the control classes, specifically the entity managers, is also important in order to effectively support distributed transaction tasks. If well designed, they can integrate seamlessly with .NET's transaction control capabilities.

■ Entity classes represent the business concepts manipulated by the system and are the basic blocks of control for the information that must be persisted (although not all entities need persistence). Entity classes and their relationships constitute the basis for the logical design of the database. In most situations, entity classes are not specific to a use case and often not even specific to the system itself, but they are used by all the enterprise systems. Entity classes can only communicate with control classes, in particular entity managers, which will ensure the maintenance of the integrity of the relationships between the related entity classes. All communication to entities should be organized though an entity manager. This may result in an apparent duplication of responsibilities, where an entity manager just delegates the responsibility to one of its managed entities. Nevertheless, it is a good practice to use this approach, which helps to effectively achieve decoupling between presentation, business, and data access layers. A concrete example of the importance of entity managers is to consider what happens when the entity's operations need to support transactions. The best place to define transaction logic involving entities is in the corresponding entity manager, which has the best knowledge of how entities relate and operate, as opposed to having this knowledge and logic scattered in all layers of the system.

The static part of the model is contained in the Key Abstractions package. Within this package, you create one package per use case package, as in the use case model. Within each of these packages, you define three subpackages: Boundary, Control, and Entity.

Boundary Classes

In this section we will consider the boundary classes that represent user interface elements. You will find in the Case Study section of this chapter, as well as in Chapter 6, a discussion of a boundary class representing an external system adapter. In the context of user interface modeling, the Boundary package's goal is to receive all classes that represent user interface elements. At this level of detail, these classes can just be the corresponding screens in the user experience model. The simplest and most sufficient approach is to create boundary classes for each screen of the user experience model. You do not need to duplicate the attributes and operations, as the analysis model will not make use of actual class operations in the sequence diagrams.

Allocate the boundary classes in the analysis model structure the same way as in the user experience model. The attributes and operations of the screen classes will serve to directly define the Web pages and controls in the detailed design. This is also true for the input forms, which are not transposed to the analysis model, as they are supposed to be part of a screen. You complete this approach by creating a traceability diagram, to formally establish the one-to-one relationship between boundary classes in the analysis model and screens in the user experience model, as depicted in Figure 5-4. In this diagram you can also represent the input forms owned by the screens. This will be useful later on in detailed design, to help you keep track of the input forms and their attributes and operations, which you need to represent in some form in the design classes that will model the screens and input forms.

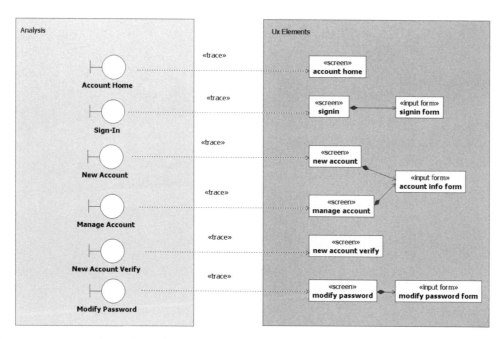

Figure 5-4: Tracing boundary classes to screens for the User Account Management package.

Control Classes

The next package to consider, within a specific use case package, is the Control package. The activity here is to identify candidate control classes, and the practical approach to this problem is to:

- Define a control class for each use case, named after the use case name suffixed with "Dispatcher" (e.g., for Create Account, "Create Account Dispatcher"). This kind of control class will control the flow of execution for a specific use case. Note that later in the analysis you may find that it makes sense to merge two or more of these control classes into one.

- Create a control class for each use case package, named after the package name suffixed with "Manager" (e.g., for User Account Management, "User Account Manager" or simply "Account Manager" as per the case study). This kind of control class will manage the related entities for the package, which can be found in the Entity subpackage.

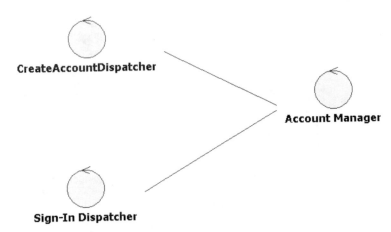

CreateAccountDispatcher

Account Manager

Sign-In Dispatcher

Figure 5-5: Associations between control classes in the User Account Management package.

You can also represent the associations between control classes within a specific use case package, as depicted in Figure 5-5. This will serve as reference for the design of the View of Participating Classes (VOPC) diagrams.

Entity Classes

The last package to define is the Entity package, where you identify classes holding information that most likely needs to be saved in a persistent data store. Note, however, that in some cases entities may represent temporary objects that don't need persistence. The initial list of entities can be derived from the business entity model, which in turn is the subset of the business object model, where only the business entities are considered, as depicted in Figure 5-6 for the Customer Management organizational unit.

From this model, we create the initial entity model, and we look to augment it and further specify it by reviewing the use case details. This work results in a more accurate entity model like the one presented in Figure 5-7. As you recall from the business modeling activity, the only possible relationships between business entities are generic aggregation, association, and generalization. You may notice that in Figure 5-7 the class relationships have been refined, as we decided in the analysis that the generic aggregation between the User and Credit Card entities is actually a composition. Note also that the enti-

Figure 5-6: Business entities for the Customer Management organizational unit.

ties are all sitting within a frame named "Account Manager," thus making it clear that these entities are managed by the corresponding entity manager.

As noted earlier, ideally the entity model is common to all enterprise systems and links all the system functions. For this reason, it is important to also present all the entities in one diagram, named the Managed Entities diagram, as in Figure 5-8. The name of this diagram stems from the fact that all entities

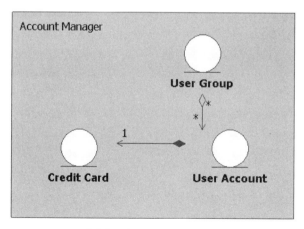

Figure 5-7: Entity model for the User Account Management package.

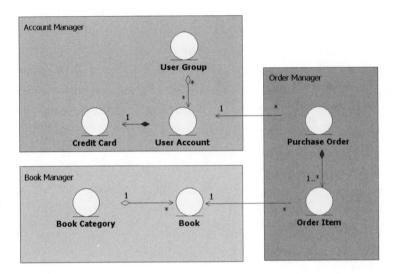

Figure 5-8: Managed Entities diagram.

are organized in clusters under the control class that has the responsibility to manage them.

In Figure 5-8 you can notice three types of associations:

- Unspecified associations (e.g., between Purchase Order and User Account). This type of association is useful when relating entities that are in the realm of two separate entity managers. Both ends of the associations have to specify their multiplicities.

- Aggregation associations (e.g., between User Group and User Account). Use this type of association to convey more specific semantics about the relationship. Aggregation describes a situation where one class is part of another, while the part class may belong to more than one aggregate class. In the example, a User Account is part of one or more User Groups. Both ends of the associations have to specify their multiplicities.

- Composition associations (e.g., between User Account and Credit Card). This type of association denotes an even stronger relationship, where one class is composed (is the whole) of the part class, while the part class cannot belong to any other composition. The parts live and die with the whole, which means that when the composing class has to be deleted, the parts also have to be deleted; the classes are either stored in permanent storage or not. In the example, a User Account is composed of one and only one Credit Card and each Credit Card is part of only one User Account. When the User Account is discarded, the attached Credit Card should also be discarded. In this type of association, the multiplicity of the composing class is always 1, thus it is not represented in the model.

Here is an important remark about the attributes of the entity classes of the analysis model. These attributes are not represented in this model, but for the entities that stem from the business object model, they are specified as part of the definition of the business entity within the business glossary, and can be carried on to the design model. For other entities that are discovered during the specification of the analysis model, these entities have to be defined in the system glossary, with any attributes that can be identified at this stage of the process. In the same way as for the business entities, their attributes will be carried on and will be further refined in the detailed design as part of creating the database design model.

View of Participating Classes Diagram

The dynamic part of the model is contained within the Use Case Realization package. In this package you find one use case realization per use case, as depicted earlier in Figure 5-2. Use case realizations are the transposition, in terms of object collaborations, of a use case scenario, which is defined as one specific instance of the flow of events of a use case. As with the storyboards, you find two elements for each use case realization: one or more sequence diagrams and a VOPC diagram.

The VOPC diagram is central to the analysis model. When trying to go from the *What* of a use case to the *How* of the system design, the basic question asked is, What are all the system objects involved in the realization of a use case? You get an idea of the answer to this question by examining the business entity model and the user experience model, but the VOPC diagram is the first class diagram of the system to show a complete and comprehensive set of system objects collaborating in the context of one use case. Note that at this level of abstraction, the system objects are described as analysis classes.

You create this diagram by combining the boundary, control, and entity classes that are involved for the realization of the use case, as presented in Figure 5-9. The primary source for the classes involved are the classes found in the Key Abstraction use case package, which corresponds to the package owning the realized use case; for example, for the Create Account use case realization, you take a subset of the classes under the User Account Management package, in the Key Abstractions package. After creating an initial VOPC diagram with these classes, you will add any other classes that you identify to take part in the use case realization. The VOPC diagram should present all the objects involved in the use case, not only for the basic flow but also for all the alternate flows.

An important note on VOPC diagrams is that you can use simple, nondirected associations between the classes involved (with the exception of the relationships between entity classes). The rationale behind this approach is that you do not gain much by specifying the associations, while you take the risk of spending too much time to decide if an association is unidirectional or bidirectional. Remember that the VOPC diagrams, as well as the whole

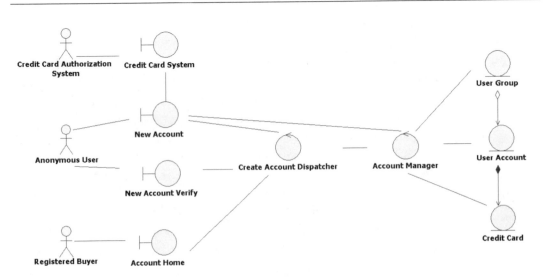

Figure 5-9: VOPC diagram for the Create Account use case.

analysis model, should avoid too much detail. Besides, you can safely defer this kind of decision until the detailed design or even until the implementation.

Sequence Diagrams

The initial VOPC diagram is the primary source of objects for the sequence diagrams of the corresponding use case realization. The sequence diagram, as depicted in Figure 5-10, represents the collaboration of an actor and the system objects involved in the realization of the task represented by the use case.

This collaboration is represented in UML by messages that are exchanged between classes. These messages represent the responsibilities of the classes and will turn into operations in the design model. There is one sequence diagram for each possible use case scenario of interest you identify. Sequence diagrams represent use case scenarios or a step-by-step description of a complete path through the use case. In practice, you define a use case scenario for each flow of events identified in the corresponding use case; you should create at least the sequence diagram corresponding to the basic flow of events of each use case. Beyond this mechanical definition of use case scenarios, you should also consider any alternate scenario that is of interest for the system test activity.

It is important to understand that this is the very point in the process where you define the system tests, and in Chapter 9 we will use the use case scenarios as input into the design of the test cases. It is also interesting to note that the testing concerns are addressed very early in the process and that the testing activity directly relates to the modeling. When deciding the use case scenarios to design, you should really think of what you need to properly test the system. You will find an interesting technique to identify all possible use case scenarios in the magazine article "Generating Test Cases from Use Cases." The principle of the technique is to combine one or more flows of events into a use case scenario, considering all possible combinations of flows of events. Note that in each use case scenario you have one part of the basic flow of events, up to the point of the first alternate flow selected for the specific use case scenario.

In the analysis model the classes are not specified with attributes and operations, so the messages that you define on these diagrams do not correspond to operations in the associated classes. Thus, you preserve the high-level nature

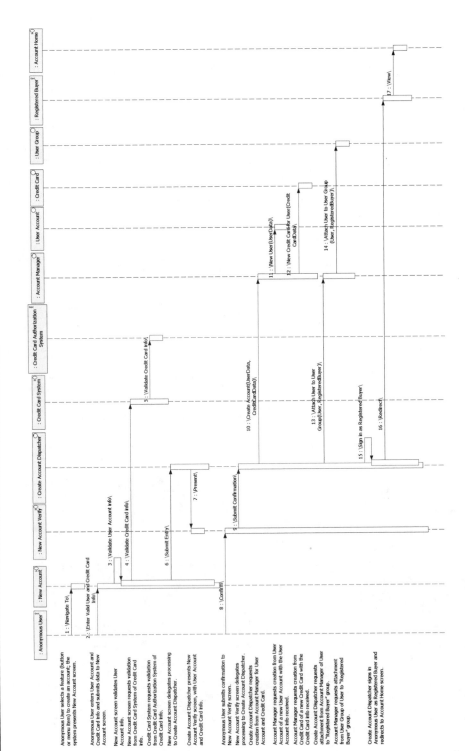

Figure 5-10: Sequence diagram for the Create Account use case.

of the analysis model, while not thinking too much about the details, and at the same time you create a starting point for defining operations in the design model.

Considering both the VOPC and sequence diagrams, you may notice that they effectively comprise the user experience elements of the user experience model, along with other system objects. This clarifies the fact that the analysis model is the glue between the use case model and the user experience model.

An interesting technique to apply is to reformulate the use case text as a narrative of the sequence of messages, on the left side of the sequence diagram. The objective here is to create a textual description, equivalent to the use case description, but which explicitly references the system objects involved in the interaction, as identified in the use case realization's VOPC diagram. You can then use these narratives to validate the use case description and, if necessary, amend it, while possibly discovering new objects that can be elevated to the rank of business objects. While it may sometimes seem awkward to try to use the noun-verb-noun construct in the use case, using it in the sequence diagram narratives is not only easier, it is also important if you want to be able to use the narrative as the link between the use cases and the VOPC diagram.

This approach makes sense when you think that the analysis model is the first step in describing *How* the system will implement the specifications; that is, the *What* of the use cases. Indeed, these narratives take the point of view of describing *How* the system works, thus effectively realizing the *What* in the context of the technological choices of the solution.

Case Study

Key Abstractions—Managed Entities

By applying the principles presented in the Approach to the Case Study, we will produce an analysis model that will cover the use case realization of the Create Account use case.

As for every other activity in the process, the core input artifact for the analysis is the Create Account use case, which you can review in Appendix D. In Figure 5-1 you can review the structure of the analysis model, from the point of view of the realization of the Create Account use case. Tracing of the artifacts is presented in Figure 5-2, where you can identify the user experience storyboard, which you need to use as the source of information on the boundary classes. In Figure 5-6 you can find the part of the business object model containing the business entities involved in the Create Account function. These business entities will be used to initiate the entity model. For completion, the part of the use case model that involves the Create Account use case may be reviewed in Figure 5-11.

Start by defining the Boundary package, using as input the screen elements found in the corresponding package of the user experience model. As per the Approach, at this stage it is sufficient to have a one-to-one mapping between boundary classes and the screens in that package, as presented previously with the traceability diagram of Figure 5-4. Reviewing the use case model, you can see that the Create Account use case involves some interaction with the Credit Card Authorization System. But, as you recall from Chapter 3, using this type of actor, who represents external systems, will result in the definition of an adapter boundary class, in order to easily integrate within the underlying technology used for the solution (that is, .NET). You thus have to define an additional boundary class in the analysis model, "Credit Card System"; the best approach is also to put it in a separate package, the "Credit Card System" package as depicted earlier in Figure 5-1.

The responsibilities of this boundary class will be defined by the capabilities of the interface that the external system supports. In the adapter boundary class you should consider wrapping only the capabilities that are of use for the system you develop. You may also be lucky enough to find that the external

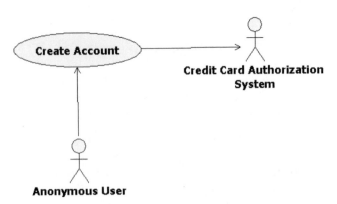

Figure 5-11: Use case model: The Create Account use case perspective.

system has already implemented an interface integrated with .NET, so that this interface plays the role of the boundary class. In the analysis model, you should still model a boundary class, because you are not allowed to have a control class communicating directly with an actor. Later on, in the detailed design, you will have to make a choice about how to represent the interaction with the external system. This will be discussed in Chapter 6.

Defining the Control package is equally simple. Define a dispatcher type of control class, "Create Account Dispatcher," to control the flow of execution of the use case. Create also an entity manager type of control class, "Account Manager," to manage the entities of the whole use case package. This mechanical approach of identifying control classes defines an analysis pattern where, for each use case, you need to define the collaboration between one dispatcher and one entity manager control class.

Thus, the two control classes communicate with each other, as presented in the class diagram of Figure 5-5. The nonmechanical part of the job will come later, when you need to define the responsibilities of the control classes. A first cut will be achieved when creating the sequence diagram of the use case, where the analysis of the use case will help you identify the broad responsibilities of each control class. Dispatcher control classes will be assigned responsibilities based on the analysis of the flow of events, while entity manager control classes will be assigned responsibilities based on which entities are involved in the use case and what their roles are.

The specification of the Entity package involves a mechanical approach, but also some analysis of the use case. The mechanical part is about identifying the part of the model covering the function represented by the use case in the business object model. In practice, you will be looking for the part of the business object model covering the function defined by the use case package where the use case belongs (e.g., for the Create Account use case, look for the business object model covering the User Account Management function). Recalling Chapter 2, this is the Customer Management organization unit.

In the business model we identify two entities, User Account and Credit Card, as presented previously in Figure 5-6. You can verify that these entities are also referenced in the use case description. But at this stage of the process, you should also try to refine the entity relationships. By examining the business glossary for the definition of these entities, you notice that the User Account indeed owns a Credit Card. You should represent this refined information on the analysis entity model, by specifying a composition relationship between the two entities, as depicted earlier in Figure 5-7.

Continuing the analysis of the use case text, you notice the following sentence: "The system also allocates the user to the group of Registered Buyers, and stores this information in relation with the User Account." What this sentence says is that the system has to manage some information related to which group the user belongs to, and we can define a new entity to support this management. We name this entity "User Group," and we must define its attributes—logically, "group name" and "group description." This definition has to go in the system glossary, because it has not been identified as a useful concept at the level of abstraction of the business glossary. A User Group entity can reference zero or more User Account entities, or you can say that a User Group aggregates zero or more User Accounts. Thus, you can represent this relationship by an aggregation association, as depicted previously in Figure 5-7. Table 5-1 is an excerpt of the system glossary for our small business example. This system glossary is complete relative to the Create Account use case description.

Table 5-1: System glossary excerpt.

Term	Definition
Buyer	Buyer is any type of Actor who can browse the book catalogue and add items to a shopping cart.
Registered User	Registered User is any type of Actor who has an account on the system.
Anonymous User	Anonymous User is an Actor who is not registered and can only browse the catalogue, adding items to a shopping cart, but cannot place orders. They are a special type of Buyer.
Registered Buyer	Registered Buyer is an Actor who has an account on the system and can place orders. They are a special type of Buyer and also a Registered User. This Actor is listed in a User Group named "Registered Buyer."
Administrator	Administrator is an Actor who has an account on the system, can act as a Registered Buyer, but can also manage the accounts that are listed in the User Group named "Registered Buyer." They are a special type of Registered Buyer. This Actor is listed in a User Group named "Admin."
User Group	User Group information includes the following: ■ Group Name. ■ Group Description.

Note that, from the above work, you have created an entity model where all entities are managed by only one entity manager control class, namely Account Manager, as depicted in Figure 5-7. Thus, this figure presents the Create Account perspective of the more general Managed Entities diagram, presented in Figure 5-8, which holds all the entities of the system, along with their entity manager control classes.

View of Participating Classes Diagram

Having identified the basic set of analysis classes involved in the realization of the Create Account use case, you can present them all within the initial participants diagram of the use case realization, as depicted earlier in Figure 5-9.

Sequence Diagrams

With the VOPC diagram you can jump straight to the definition of the sequence diagrams for the various use case scenarios, starting with the one covering the basic flow of events. Lay on top of the sequence diagram all the objects found in the VOPC diagram. The next step is very important and consists of reformulating the basic flow of events of the Create Account use case. Review the use case and describe the basic flow of events in terms of the objects of the VOPC diagram, using the construct of noun-verb-noun. Nouns are actors, boundary and entity classes in the VOPC diagram. Verbs will represent responsibilities of the control classes. Table 5-2 shows the flow of events revisited to fit this specification:

When reformulating the use case description, you have to ask yourself the following basic questions: Is that description equivalent to the one in the use case? Can I be assured that it does not define more information? Does it define less information? If, when answering these questions, you can point to an element that is not equivalent, you have to revisit the use case and make it consistent with this description.

You can now directly attach the above, reformulated text as the narrative on the left side of the sequence diagram. Each step can translate to a message, thus creating a mapping between the message number and the steps of the narrative. The resulting sequence diagram for the basic flow of the Create Account use case was presented earlier in Figure 5-10.

Table 5-2: Basic flow of events.

Step	Description
1.	Anonymous User selects a feature (button or menu item) to create an account; the system presents New Account screen.
2.	Anonymous User enters User Account and Credit Card info and submits data to New Account screen.
3.	New Account screen validates User Account info.
4.	New Account screen requests validation from Credit Card System of Credit Card info.
5.	Credit Card System requests validation from Credit Card Authorization System of Credit Card info.
6.	New Account screen delegates processing to Create Account Dispatcher.
7.	Create Account Dispatcher presents New Account Verify screen, with User Account and Credit Card info.
8.	Anonymous User submits confirmation to New Account Verify screen.
9.	New Account Verify screen delegates processing to Create Account Dispatcher.
10.	Create Account Dispatcher requests creation from Account Manager for User Account and Credit Card.
11.	Account Manager requests creation from User Account of a new User Account with the User Account info received.
12.	Account Manager requests creation from Credit Card of a new Credit Card with the Credit Card info received.
13.	Create Account Dispatcher requests attachment from Account Manager of User to "Registered Buyer" group.
14.	Account Manager requests attachment from User Group of User to "Registered Buyer" group.
15.	Create Account Dispatcher signs in Anonymous User as Registered Buyer and redirects to Account Home screen.

Note the way we represent the role change from Anonymous User to Registered Buyer on the diagram. A more direct way of presenting it would be with a "Navigate To" message from "Create Account Dispatcher" to "Account Home," as depicted in Figure 5-12.

The rationale for presenting the interaction through the "Registered User" actor has to do with the role-based security design. As you will see in Chapter 8, adopting the representation of Figure 5-12 implies that the "Anonymous

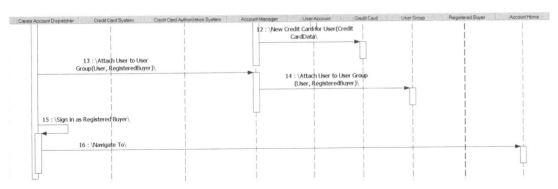

Figure 5-12: An alternate collaboration when signing in Anonymous User.

User" role has access to the "Account Home" screen, by virtue of the "Navigate To" message being part of the overall interaction initiated by "Anonymous User." This is not what we want to express, and using the model of Figure 5-10 makes clear the fact that it is the "Registered User" role that is allowed to access that screen.

Summary

In this chapter we reviewed the activities related to the development of the analysis model, which serves as an intermediary step before detailed design, by integrating the use case and user experience model. The analysis model also proves very helpful in avoiding the analysis paralysis phenomenon, by getting a head start in developing the detailed design model. As an intermediate step, it is not meant to drill into many details, thus the class elements are not represented with any attributes or operations, and the associations are not specified. One exception is the relationship between entity classes, which will serve as the basis for the database design model.

The activities involve the production of two artifacts, the key abstractions, which also define the managed entities, and use case realizations, which in turn consist of the sequence diagrams and the VOPC diagram. The analysis model deals with the following analysis classes: boundary, control, and entity.

The Managed Entities diagram represents all the persistent entities of the system, and ideally it is used for all the systems within an enterprise. Entity relationships are all specified to the best of the knowledge and understanding of the designers, and this part of the model can be directly used for the database design model.

Within the use case realization you create one VOPC diagram and define at least one use case scenario for the basic flow of events of the use case. For each use case scenario you create one sequence diagram. The selection of use case scenarios serves as the basis for the system test. Optionally, you create more sequence diagrams for use case scenarios corresponding to alternate flows of events. The sequence diagrams represent the realization of the flow of events of the use case, within the context of the system object model defined by the VOPC diagram. The messages that you define on this diagram do not correspond to operations in the associated classes. They serve as guidelines to distribute responsibilities among the classes and as a starting point for defining operations in the design model.

Within a use case realization, the sequence diagrams and VOPC diagram are also used to validate the corresponding use case description. For this, it is helpful to reformulate the use case text as a narrative on the left side of the sequence diagram. In this form, you must pay attention to not alienate the information captured in the use case, while describing it in terms of the system objects identified in the VOPC diagram.

Chapter 6

Design Model

Introduction

A better denomination for the design model would be the "detailed design model," as it is the second level of the system design. The activities involved at this stage have as an objective to define the system in such detail that there is a minimal gap to cross before producing the code. In an ideal situation, crossing that gap should be transparent to the designers and developers. This situation is achieved by the use of tools that understand the underlying technology and can generate code in the target language, as well as generate configuration settings in the technology infrastructure. In turn these tools are more likely to prove satisfactory if the underlying technology itself implements the concepts that are used in the modeling approach—that is, if it implements object-oriented principles in its very structure. And this is outstandingly the case with the .NET framework.

As we have seen in Chapter 1, the definition of software engineering has the practical implication to mandate the use of tools, techniques/methods, and processes to implement traceability. Because the realization of the vision has this dependency, we should evaluate its practical applicability by developing a measure of maturity for each of these elements. Considering the issue from this angle, we have to also consider two more elements, which extend the layers of tools at the bottom, techniques/methods at the middle, and processes at the top. These new elements are technology at the bottom and people at the top. Figure 6-1 presents the maturity elements that are most important in the efficient production of software. I have also added a sixth element, organization, measured within the framework of the Capability Maturity Model (introduced in Chapter 1).

In a cursory review of the people element, we have to consider people maturity against the four elements underneath it. The questions asked here are, Are people mature in using the new technological platforms? Are people mature in using advanced tools? Are people mature in using the techniques and methods promoted? Are people mature in abiding by standard processes?

But in this book we are more interested in the implication of the technology in the software engineering vision. The maturity of the technology element can simply be evaluated against:

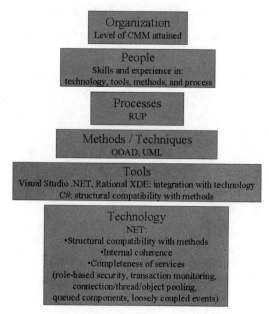

Figure 6-1: Elements of maturity for the efficient production of software.

- Its structural compatibility with the methods used (OOAD).

- Its completeness in terms of services offered (e.g., transactions, queued components, role-based security, and object and thread pooling). This functional coverage of infrastructure issues will determine to what degree the application designer is immune to the need of developing such elements, which obviously do not fall within the concerns of a business automation solution.

- Its internal coherence, which is defined by how well designed the interfaces to the infrastructure services are, and the collaborations of the services with each other.

Even a cursory review of the *Microsoft .NET Framework SDK* documentation will be sufficient to convince you of its maturity in the above perspective. This maturity can also be easily verified for the development tools that integrate with this platform. First, considering the C# language, you will find that its structure is tightly fitted to support the .NET framework structure. The same remark is applicable for Microsoft Visual Studio .NET, with a list of features that match the capabilities and structure of the .NET framework.

In this chapter I will review the activities of creating the design model in relation with some activities of coding in Microsoft Visual Studio .NET. As the focus of this book is not in describing either the .NET framework or the Microsoft Visual Studio .NET environment, the subsequent discussion will assume that you have a working knowledge of these elements. You will also find in the Bibliography a few book references that cover all aspects of .NET.

Approach

Guiding Principles

The overall approach followed in the design activity stems from the fact that, as presented in the Introduction, the objective is to create a detailed design of the system. As a consequence, we can define a certain number of guiding principles:

- All classes should be specified to the level of detail that they represent implementation classes. In fact, the design model will serve as a container of diagrams, referencing implementation classes, with the purpose of describing their collaborations. At the same time, all implementation classes should be represented in a model.

- A sequence diagram should be defined for each flow of events documented in each use case.

- Because of the previous two principles, all messages in sequence diagrams should represent actual operations. Only in special situations should you permit the use of descriptive messages. This is most likely to be the case with the messages describing user actions on user interface classes, but other situations may also need to use descriptive messages.

- You should avoid representing in the diagrams the classes of the underlying .NET technological framework. The collaboration of the solution classes with the .NET framework is an implementation concern and will be addressed in the code. On the other hand, you may judge that the clarity of the model will benefit from the representation of some of the .NET classes. This is more likely to be the case when describing architecturally significant design mechanisms, as these mechanisms often address complex architectural issues, which need to be well understood as they have a broad impact on the system.

- An important objective in the design model is to achieve class cohesiveness. Class cohesiveness is defined as a measure of the efficiency of the interclass communication, and you should strive to produce designs that minimize this communication. A practical implication of cohesiveness is in the performance of distributed systems. Interclass communication is always slower when crossing machine or network boundaries than within the same machine. Class cohesiveness yields one of the most visible advantages of developing a model of the code. It is very difficult to detect noncohesive classes by looking at the code, while it appears obvious in sequence diagrams when you notice an excessive amount of messages that are needed to complete one action. Putting these considerations in the perspective of the software engineering vision, a good design gives you confidence in the performance of the system, before any performance testing is conducted.

Assumptions and Constraints

As this book is meant to present a practical approach to system design, I will take the liberty of making some assumptions and imposing a few constraints on the way I expect a modern team to apply a software engineering approach to development. These assumptions and constraints relate mainly to the use of adequate tools to support the software development process and define an approach to address the practical implications of the software engineering vision, as defined and described in Chapter 1:

- I will assume the usage of a design tool that defines a round-trip engineering environment. That means that the design tool is able to generate code from a model, as well as represent in the model the classes and structure found in .NET source code. Thus, the model is a visual representation of the code. This assumption is a practical necessity in order to support the guiding principle of producing complete and detailed design of all the implementation classes.

- I will assume that the design tool supports the semantics of all the .NET framework concepts, as defined in the Common Language Specification library. As a reminder, all .NET-compatible languages have to support the same set of architecture constructs, thus achieving the interoperability of .NET components created with any .NET language. The semantics being the same, only the names of the language constructs differ from one language to another. The design tools can support the .NET semantics by using UML stereotypes and some UML extensions. In Chapter 7, you will see how the .NET elements of assemblies, namespaces, and files can be represented in the model using stereotyped UML elements.

- The persistent storage capability shall rely on a relational database. The consequence of this constraint is that we also need to define a database model for the data access.

The above assumptions are minimalist in the sense that most design tools today are expected to support them. One way to use a design tool such as the one described above is to precisely define in the tool all the details of the classes and then request the tool to generate the code. If the tool is of satisfactory precision, the code generated will support the correct semantics from the model and compile without error. The reality is that proceeding this way is tedious and time-consuming, as it is not very natural to use the design tool to define every class, every operation signature, every input and output parameter.

To alleviate this apparent burden imposed by the tool, a much more practical approach, based on the assumptions above, is to create the code structure first using Microsoft Visual Studio .NET, and then use the reverse-engineering features of the design tool to create the class definitions in the models. A tool like Rational XDE has an additional feature that enables you to continually synchronize the code with the model. At this stage you are only concerned with the class structure, thus you write the code for the definition of the classes, their attributes, their getters and setters, and their operations. By defining at the same time the code and the sequence diagrams that describe the collaborations of the code elements, you are able to effectively achieve consistency between the design and the code. After all, the code is just one more level of abstraction in the representation of the knowledge.

Note that in this approach, you have to define an initial implementation model before starting the design, and in Chapter 7 I will discuss a technique for doing so. To ensure that you keep the model consistent with the code and as a matter of best practice, you should only be concerned with reverse engineering of the code to the implementation model, with the design model referencing implementation classes, as described earlier. The practical approach described does not mandate the use of forward code-generation capabilities of the modeling tool (although it does not prevent it, either). Thus, you are always free to use the modeling tool in order to make changes in the implementation model and then generate the code. Note, however, that for the database model, the approach makes use of both reverse-engineering and forward database definition capabilities of the modeling tool.

Model Structure

The design model is a second, detailed level of specification of the analysis model. As such, every structural element of the design model should be traced to one or more elements of the analysis model. By structural elements, you should understand the class definitions. As you recall from Chapter 5, in the analysis model we do not specify the attributes and operations of the classes. In the case of boundary classes representing screens and input forms, the attributes and operations are carried over from the user experience model to the design model. In the case of entity classes, the attributes and operations stem from the definition of the entities in the glossaries. Thus, the basis of the design model is the analysis model, and you need to consider it in each of its static and dynamic parts.

An important thing to understand is that we do not expect to identify more system classes than we already have in the analysis model. At least the probability of such an event is quite low, as a well-designed analysis model should have unveiled most of the classes; the View Of Participating Classes (VOPC) diagrams play a very important role in this perspective. Thus, the initial set of classes of the design model is exactly the same as in the analysis model.

The structure of the model, as depicted in Figure 6-2, makes a broad separation between design elements that define common architecturally significant mechanisms, and Business packages that structure the design elements around reusable subsystems that implement business logic.

The Business packages follow the same borders defined by the organization of use cases in packages, seen in the analysis model. In Figure 6-2, you have the following three Business packages: Maintenance, Store Front, and User Account Management. This structure mirrors the Use Case Realization package of the analysis model. Following also the same principles as for the analysis model, each Business package aims at realizing the use cases that fall within its realm. Thus, under each Business package you can find a Use Case Realization package, containing all the associated use case realizations, as depicted in Figure 6-2.

This package structures the use cases of the Business package, with each use case defining a number of sequence diagrams that describe the collaboration of the elements in the context of the specific use case. Because Business packages contain the realization of use cases, and because a use case involves presentation, business, and data access elements, each Business package is further structured along the packages stereotyped "layer" that focuses on the static representation of each aspects of the elements involved.

In the example above, you can notice that the Store Front Business package has a business layer composed of two subsystems: Book Management and Order Management. Using a subsystem element in place of a package is important, as these elements have different semantics, with a subsystem being a specialization of a package. A subsystem provides behavior through one or more interfaces that it realizes, while a package is just a container of other elements.

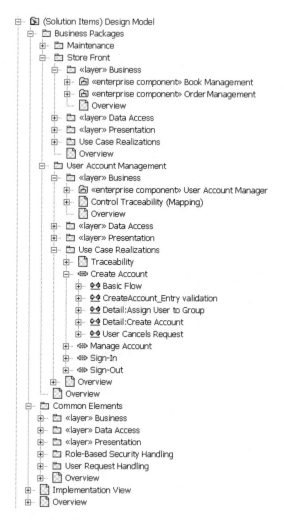

Figure 6-2: Design model structure.

The above subsystems are stereotyped as enterprise components, as their aim is to be reused for the development of every system within the enterprise. This is achieved by virtue of defining these subsystems around the entity managers identified in the analysis model, as shown in Figure 6-3, in the Managed Entities diagram of the analysis model. The rationale behind this approach is

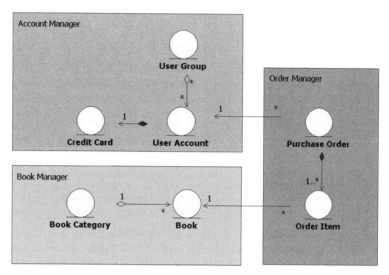

Figure 6-3: Managed entities.

that the managed entities are themselves supposed to be common to all enterprise systems, as discussed in Chapter 5. While the analysis model defines a logical organization of functionality into Business packages, the design model defines a logical organization of components into enterprise components.

From the discussion so far, it appears that the best way to start the design model is to create its overall structure, which is a fairly mechanical step, as you just need to apply the principles above.

There is one more reason to start by defining the model structure. As described in the assumptions, there is a dependency that the implementation model be defined before starting the specification of the design model. As you will see in Chapter 7, the creation of the implementation model uses the design model structure as a starting point. Thus, at this stage the process prompts you to first create the implementation model before continuing with the rest of the approach. For the remainder of this chapter you should assume that the implementation model is available. In Chapter 7 you will also find that the design model is the best place to hold the implementation view, hence the existence of that diagram as presented at the bottom of Figure 6-2.

Data Access Layer and .NET Strongly Typed DataSets

The next step is to concentrate on the data model for the whole system. As described in Chapter 5, the Managed Entities diagram represents all the entities of the solution, with all their relationships. This diagram also clusters the entities around their respective entity manager, as depicted in Figure 6-3. As mentioned in Chapter 5, ideally the entity model is common to all enterprise systems and is the basis for creating the data model. In Figure 6-3 you can also notice that entities can have associations with entities controlled by other entity managers, thus the entities involved in the realization of one specific use case may depend on entities that are not part of the participant entities of the use case, as defined by the use case VOPC diagram. In other words, every use case may possibly depend on the totality of the entity model and not on the specific subset identified in the associated VOPC diagram. All the associations between entities will be realized as some type of relationship in the database model.

It is very important to note that when an entity has an association with another entity that is managed by a different entity manager, this association will be managed between the two entity managers and not between the two entities or between the entity manager of one entity and the associated entity. In other words, the entity manager of one entity will request the services of the entity manager of the second entity in order to make changes or retrieve information for the associated entity that is outside its boundary of control. In the database model, these associations will be realized with nonidentifying relationships (see the following "Database Design Model" section).

Because of the interconnection of the entities beyond the boundaries of entity managers, the first activity of the detail design consists of detailing the entity model and creating the data model for all the entities of the system. In reality, because the system is developed based on iterations, you might not define in the current iteration the complete entity model, but only the subset identified in the use case analysis of the current iteration. At the same time you have a very good approximation of the totality of the entities by considering the business object model. You should keep in mind the possibility that in later iterations you may have to change the current entity model, when other parts of the analysis model will be developed and new entities or relationships will be unveiled.

In modeling the data access part of the model, we shall apply a design pattern which, though of general applicability, is especially important in order to take advantage of some .NET data access features defined in ADO.NET. As the title of the book indicates, we are concerned with design for .NET, and we shall not hesitate to use all the powerful features available in that framework. The general idea of the pattern is to separate two concerns of the Data Access Layer:

- The data itself, as classes containing only the information that pertains to one specific entity. These classes are common to every solution within the realm of the entity model. We shall refer to them as the Data Type classes. Conceptually, these classes are structured documents containing the associated business type information, and they are exchanged between all other classes of the system, which you can conceptualize as workers. Defining these classes as structured documents will immediately make it clear that we should use XML syntax for their representation. Thus, the class structure itself and the relationships with other Data Type classes will be expressed in some sort of schema definition, such as XML Schema.

- The set of the specific operations that is defined on the data for the specific needs of our solution. These classes will define the Data Access Layer and are specific to the solution. We will refer to them as the Data Layer classes or Data Access Layer classes. Modeling (with sequence diagrams) their collaborations with other classes of the solution will help you discover the set of operation they implement. At least they should exhibit the standard set of CRUD operations (Create, Retrieve, Update, and Delete).

Collectively we will refer to these two sets of classes as Data Access classes. The result of the application of this pattern is presented in Figure 6-4.

The above definition of Data Type classes is of general applicability. But using XML documents to exchange data between classes is not practical because each class has then to implement XML document manipulation. To address this problem, a sensible approach consists of defining for each Data Type class a wrapper class that would implement generic CRUD functionality (as opposed to specific functionality of the Data Layer classes), as well as getters and setters for the attributes representing the business type information.

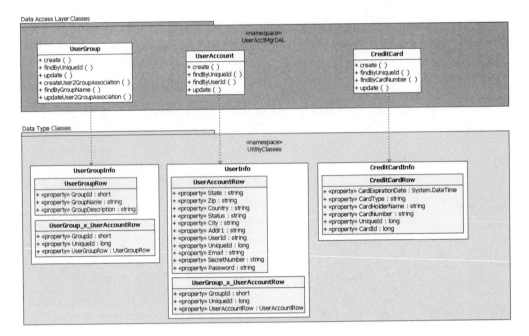

Figure 6-4: Data Access classes for User Account Management.

What you would end up with is a strongly typed XML document, as it is represented by a class encapsulating the XML document and the schema definition.

This was the way I used to design XML-based data access before .NET. Not anymore, thanks to ADO.NET and the concept of strongly typed DataSets, which do exactly what is described above: define Data Type classes with all the wiring included. You can see this in Figure 6-4 above, where you can notice how we take advantage of the ADO.NET DataSets, for the Data Type classes. The UserGroupInfo Data Type class represents an ADO.NET DataSet involving two tables of the database, namely the UserGroup and UserGroup_x_UserAccount tables. It also supports the relationship defined between these two tables. Later in this chapter you will find how this relationship can be represented with an XML schema file (.xsd) in Microsoft Visual Studio .NET, which will support the generation of the ADO.NET strongly typed DataSets that will correspond to the Data Type classes.

The power of ADO.NET comes from the fact that it is a redesign of ADO in two dimensions:

- Structural, to exhibit more comprehensive and cohesive interfaces and the possibility to create strongly typed DataSets.
- Technological, to completely support distributed systems. This is achieved by the generalized use of disconnected DataSets.

As a consequence of the above approach, all objects in the system manipulate strongly typed DataSets, which represent the Data Type classes together with their relationships, as described previously. DataSets can really be seen as XML documents exchanged throughout the system, especially because ADO.NET DataSets have a dual substance and are also represented as XML documents when exchanged between distributed objects over an HTTP connection.

These XML documents can be rehydrated into DataSets based on the XSD description that carries the definition of their structure and relationships. It is important to note that the class operations of strongly typed DataSets are not defined by a design activity, but by a Microsoft Visual Studio .NET generation mechanism. The only design activity involved is in defining the XML Schema of these DataSets, which is done with a special Microsoft Visual Studio .NET designer. The result is represented in Figure 6-5.

Thus, strongly typed DataSets should be considered as infrastructure classes, and you should avoid representing them within sequence diagrams, where only Data Layer classes should be represented. The Data Layer classes delegate the CRUD operations to the strongly typed DataSets. The collaboration between Data Layer classes and strongly typed DataSets is realized in the code implementation of the CRUD operations of the Data Layer classes.

The strongly typed DataSets enable the access to the database. The immediate questions that spring to mind are, How do you produce these strongly typed DataSets and How do you represent them in the model? The following section will show you a practical technique to follow, in four steps:

1. Create a database design model and generate the database definition into a database.

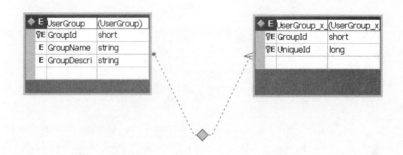

Figure 6-5: XML Schema designer in Microsoft Visual Studio .NET, with the definition of a strongly typed DataSet.

2. Use the XML Schema feature of Microsoft Visual Studio .NET to import the table definitions into XSD files. Optionally you may find it useful to tweak the definitions. In that case you should be careful to keep the consistency with the database definition.

3. Use the MSDataSetGenerator tool to generate the strongly typed DataSets into C# code files.

4. Use the reverse-engineering capabilities of the design tool to generate the model of these classes in the implementation model.

Database Design Model

As presented earlier, the persistent storage will be a relational database, which implies that we need to define a database design model. This model deals mainly with the following concepts: tables, views, domains, primary keys, foreign keys, table relationships, stored procedures, key constraints, unique constraints, triggers, indexes, and identity columns. I shall not review in this book any concept related to the physical storage of the database, such as schemas, tablespaces, and databases.

We already have defined an entity class model in the analysis phase, which represents what would be an entity-relationship model in mainstream database analysis. The question is how to go from that class model to a database design model. The technique presented here is only an example of how to tackle this issue, as this book is not meant to give an in-depth discussion on creating a database design from a UML model. You will find much more information and details on the topic in the book *UML for Database Design* (one of the features of this book is the description of the UML Profile for Database Design, which is a set of UML extensions and stereotypes to create a UML representation of the database design model).

The approach presented below entails the specification of a UML database design model as a first step, followed by the creation of the database definition within the selected RDBMS (e.g., Microsoft SQL Server). Although you can manually define the database using the RDBMS utilities, or defining a DDL script, a tool like Rational XDE supports the UML Profile for Database Design and enables you to directly create the database definition in the RDBMS by forward engineering the UML database design model. It also supports the reverse operation, which is the reverse engineering of a database definition from the RDBMS into a UML database design model, as well as the comparison and synchronization of the UML database design model with the database definition.

The advantage of this approach is that it enables you to consistently use UML to specify your system, as you are able to define and maintain the database model along with the rest of the models, particularly the implementation model that represents the code. But if you already have individuals in your team who have strong database skills and have not yet moved to the UML, or if you want to take advantage of a particular feature of your RDBMS, you may want to replace the UML database modeling step with a database design activity involving the RDBMS tools.

The database design starts from the managed entities diagram of the analysis model, as reproduced in Figure 6-3, and consists of mapping the classes and relationships to tables and relationships in the UML database design model. In this book we will consider a one-to-one mapping between classes and tables. Each instance of a class (an object) will yield the creation of a row in the table that is mapped to the entity. For the purpose of the subsequent discussion, Figure 6-6 presents the final UML database design model. As explained earlier, the column definitions of the tables come from the glossaries that hold the definition of the entities with their attributes. Note that the attribute definitions in the glossaries should be of enough detail to permit an unambiguous definition of the columns of the tables in the database design model. In this perspective it is important to specify information such as the

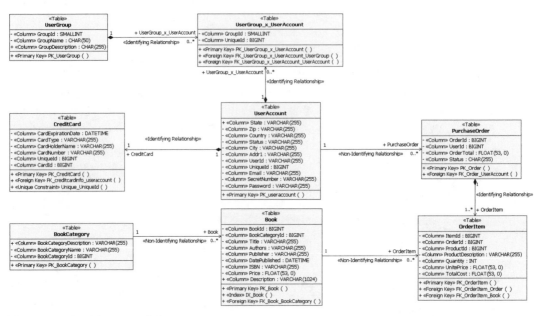

Figure 6-6: Database model.

attribute type (with the length for the text attributes) and whether it can hold a null value or not.

To support the relationships between the entities you need to choose some foreign keys. An effective way to address this issue is to define unique identifier keys for every table. Because of the one-to-one mapping between entity classes and database tables, each row in a table represents an instance of a class object. The identifying columns will then conceptually represent the unique identification of each class object. You can choose between two types of identification columns:

- Identity columns, which are generated and incremented by the database engine. Using this approach, the object identification is unique within the namespace defined by the class name. This is the approach implemented in the case study.

- Global Unique Identifier (GUID) columns, which are text columns that you will need to manage within the entity manager classes. Using this approach, the object identification is (statistically) unique within any namespace.

Composition relationships between entities are represented in the database design model by identifying relationships between tables. The implication of an identifying relationship is that the primary key of the parent table becomes part of the primary key of the child table; for example, UniqueId of UserAccount defines with CardId the primary key of the CreditCard table (presented in the FK_creditcardinfo_useraccount foreign key constraint). The semantics conveyed by this type of relationship are that a row in the child table cannot exist without a corresponding row in the parent table.

You have two choices in order to realize these semantics. The first one is to define some logic in the entity manager (Account Manager) that will maintain and enforce this constraint. This is perfectly acceptable, as we have seen earlier that all operations on related entities have to be carried out by entity managers that are aware of the intricacies of the relationships between the entities they manage.

The second approach is to realize the semantics in the database design model by defining a referential integrity constraint on the relationship, in order to enforce the deletion of the child when the parent is deleted. This will turn into a referential integrity constraint in the database definition. In the case of the relationship between UserAccount (the parent) and CreditCard (the child), a referential integrity constraint is defined on the deletion of the parent, which means that whenever a UserAccount is deleted, the corresponding CreditCard will also be deleted. This will be taken care of by the RDBMS without the need to add any logic in the entity manager (Account Manager). This second approach is simpler, as it transparently takes advantage of the capabilities of the RDBMS, without the need to define extensive logic.

As a general remark, the second approach presented above is effectively equivalent to implementing some of the business logic in the database. There are two opposing schools of thought on the question of putting business logic in the database. One says that putting a certain level of business logic in the database helps to improve performance. The other one, which is largely followed in the sample application of this book, says that putting business logic in the database results in the multiplication of forms of the representation of knowledge and thus introduces complexity in the maintenance of the system.

In general, all constraints that can be expressed in a declarative way, taking advantage of corresponding features of the RDBMS, should be expressed in the database design model, while constraints realized by stored procedures may be kept in the application logic. However, I do not hold any strong feelings in this matter, and I advise you to apply your best judgment and experience, considering issues like performance, ease of database management, and the experience of the database designers of the development team. But it is important to understand that all the business logic that you cannot or do not want to put in the database will need to be defined in the entity managers that will control the interactions with Data Access Layer classes, thus enforcing the appropriate business logic.

Considering the CreditCard entity, the entity model specifies that there is only one credit card per UserAccount. This is represented in the database design model by a unique constraint attached to the CreditCard table involving the UniqueId foreign key. You can compare this relationship with the one between PurchaseOrder and OrderItem, where you can have more than one OrderItem per PurchaseOrder. The corresponding composition also becomes an identifying relationship, but this time there is no unique constraint attached to the OrderId foreign key (presented in the FK_orderitem_order foreign key constraint).

If a many-to-many relationship is involved, you need to define an association table in the database design model. In the example of Figure 6-3, User Group and User Account define a many-to-many relationship and thus will need an association table to relate the corresponding entities in the database design model. This is represented in the database design model by the association table UserGroup_x_UserAccount. Notice the identifying relationships, which are complemented by referential integrity constraints to ensure that when a UserAccount is deleted, the corresponding entries in the association table are also deleted.

Association relationships in the entity model become nonidentifying relationships in the database design model. An example is the association between the UserAccount and the PurchaseOrder. Reviewing the entity model, this relationship goes from PurchaseOrder to UserAccount, while in the database design model it is the other way around.

The explanation of this behavior lays in the semantics of the relationship. The semantics conveyed are that the PurchaseOrder object knows which UserAccount it relates to, while the UserAccount object has no (and does not need any) direct knowledge of the PurchaseOrders that relate to it. In the database design model, by defining a nonidentifying relationship from UserAccount to PurchaseOrder, we note that the PurchaseOrder table rightly manages the foreign key of the relationship, thus reflecting the fact that the PurchaseOrder knows about UserAccount and not the other way around, realizing the semantics of the relationship defined in the entity model.

Notice that all three types of relationships in Figure 6-3 (association, aggregation, and composition) will be represented in the database design model with a foreign key relationship.

At this stage you are able to create or, ideally, generate the database definition in the target RDBMS. Having produced the database, you are able to use the XML Schema feature of Microsoft Visual Studio .NET to import the table definitions into XSD files. This can be done by first adding a new project item of type XML Schema, naming it appropriately. The convention used in the case study is to suffix the Data Layer class name by "Info" (e.g., UserGroup will become UserGroupInfo). Opening the new item in its designer, select the Server Explorer window, where you should create the appropriate connection to the database previously generated. You will be able to drag and drop the corresponding table(s) on the designer. Optionally, as for the example of the UserGroupInfo DataSet, you will also need to define a relationship between the tables, as presented earlier in Figure 6-5, and voila!, you have your XSD for one or more tables, corresponding to one Data Type class. You should also edit the XML definition to adapt the names of the elements.

Next, you have to associate "MSDataSetGenerator" to the Custom Tool property of the XML Schema item and either run the custom tool or build the project. Either way you will produce a C# code file (.cs) containing the strongly typed DataSet, with all the DataSet operations already wired. Finally, use the reverse-engineering capabilities of the design tool to generate the model of these classes in the implementation model.

At this stage you are able to represent the Data Layer classes and the Data Type classes in the Data Access diagram of Figure 6-4. This diagram represents the subset of the Data Access classes that is used for the User Account Management Business package. Notice that the diagram represented in the figure is a final diagram. At this stage of the process you are not yet able to define all operations of the Data Layer classes as it is presented on the diagram. There are some operations that you can already define: "create" to create a strongly typed DataSet; "update" to update the database with the data contained in strongly typed DataSet; and "FindByUniqueId" to retrieve a class object by it primary key, as a result of using identity columns for each table. All other operations will have to be unveiled by the activity of developing the sequence diagrams.

To be complete you also need to represent in a diagram the tracing of these classes to classes in the analysis model. This is presented in Figure 6-7, where you can notice that, because of the application of the pattern, the entity classes are realized using one Data Layer class and one Data Type class, separating the data from the operations.

The diagrams in Figures 6-4 and 6-7 are defined in the Data Access Layer package, and a detail of the structure of this package is represented in Figure 6-8. The diagrams found in this package reference classes of the implementation model, which is the reason why there are no classes defined in the

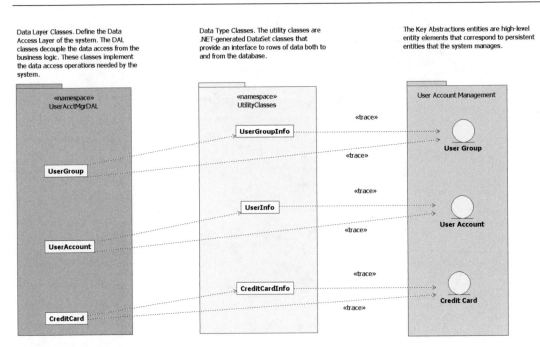

Figure 6-7: Tracing Data Access classes to analysis classes.

Figure 6-8: Structure detail of the Data Access Layer package.

package. The participants diagram is presented in Figure 6-4, and the "Entity Traceability (Mapping)" diagram is shown in Figure 6-7.

The above discussion on data access presents pretty much a mechanical way to produce the data access artifacts: design model, implementation model (Data Access classes), database design model, and code (along with the XML Schemas of the strongly typed DataSets). After creating the model structure first, these activities constitute the second important step of the design model. Within the design model structure of Figure 6-2, these activities also define the Data Access Layer packages in each of the Business packages.

Presentation Layer

The next step would be to define the presentation layer for each of the Business packages. Figure 6-9 presents the detailed structure of this package. Three diagrams are defined:

- "Boundary Traceability (Mapping)" traces back the Web forms/controls to the boundary classes in the analysis model and from there on to the screens and input forms in the user experience model.

- "Control Traceability (Mapping)" traces back dispatcher classes to the dispatcher type of control classes in the analysis model.

- "Participants" is the class diagram of the participating classes in the presentation layer (Web forms/controls and dispatchers).

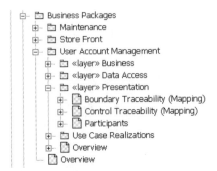

Figure 6-9: Structure detail of the Presentation Layer package.

Notice that, as for the Data Access Layer package, there are no classes defined because the diagrams reference implementation classes.

The approach for this activity is equally very mechanical, thanks to the consistent and unified approach in structuring the models. Figure 6-10 presents this equivalence of the structures.

For each Business package, you need to review in the analysis model the Control package of the corresponding Use Case Area package, in Key Abstractions (e.g., for the User Account Management package in Figure 6-9, review the Control package of the User Account Management package in the Key Abstractions package). For each analysis class that represents a dispatcher, create a code file with the definition of the class. Then, again use the reverse-

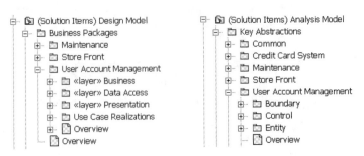

Figure 6-10: Equivalence of structures between design model and analysis model.

engineering features of the design tool to create the class definitions in the implementation model. Then you create a trace diagram for these classes, as in Figure 6-11, named "Control Traceability (Mapping)" in Figure 6-9. Note that we are not yet able to define the responsibilities of the dispatcher classes, as this will be achieved later, when creating the sequence diagrams for the use case realizations.

The boundary classes of the analysis model represent screens with input forms. These boundary classes will thus turn into .NET Web forms or Web controls in the solution, depending on the design mechanism selected. For these classes, the best approach is to create the Web forms (or controls) in Microsoft Visual Studio .NET, which will also generate the code-behind classes. The navigation elements of the forms are defined by the operations on the screen and input form classes in the user experience model. The input fields are defined by the attributes of the corresponding classes in the user experience model. By using the reverse-engineering features of the design tool, you will be able to create the corresponding class definitions in the implementation model.

Web forms in .NET help separate the page processing logic, as a C# code-behind file (.ascx.cs or .aspx.cs), and page presentation logic, as an ASP.NET

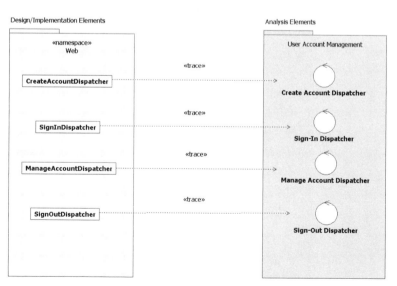

Figure 6-11: Tracing dispatcher classes to analysis classes.

file mainly containing HTML that uses some extensions in the ASP namespace (.ascx or .aspx). The page presentation file may also contain Java script to be executed locally on the browser of the client machine. The interesting thing to note with ASP.NET is that the presentation code (.ascx or .aspx) is seen as a specialization of the corresponding code-behind class, hence the "Inherits" attribute in the Control element definition (e.g., for the CreateAccount_Entry.ascx Web control file, you find in the definition: Inherits="Books REasy.Web.CreateAccount_Entry," which is in turn a code-behind class defined in CreateAccount_Entry.ascx.cs).

Because of this inheritance relationship, Microsoft Visual Studio .NET does the work of maintaining the consistency of the client and the server part of the Web form/control. These two sides can be viewed as a client and a server class. The wiring and collaboration of the two parts is also taken care of by the .NET framework. The client class (.aspx or .ascx) collaborates exclusively with its corresponding server class (.aspx.cs or .ascx.cs), but you do not need to represent this collaboration, as it is supported by the .NET framework. Only the server class, the code-behind class, will collaborate with the rest of the classes in the solution.

For this reason, modeling the client side of the Web forms/controls does not bring much in terms of understanding the collaborations between the classes involved in the realization of a use case. Thus, the screens and input forms will be represented in the implementation model by the code-behind classes of the Web forms/controls that realize them. As the code-behind files (.ascx.cs or .aspx.cs) are just plain C# code, we can rely on the reverse-engineering feature of the design tool to import their definitions in some implementation model classes.

An important diagram of the presentation layer is the diagram that traces the implementation classes to the corresponding boundary classes in the analysis model, as depicted in Figure 6-12. This diagram is named "Boundary Traceability (Mapping)" in Figure 6-9. At this stage most of the responsibilities of the Web forms/controls classes are defined, as they stem from the user experience model. Also, Microsoft Visual Studio .NET would have generated the appropriate set of default operations and attributes for these classes.

Similar to the VOPC diagram in the analysis model, a class diagram will clarify the relationships between all the classes involved in the presentation layer of a specific Business package, as presented in Figure 6-13. This diagram

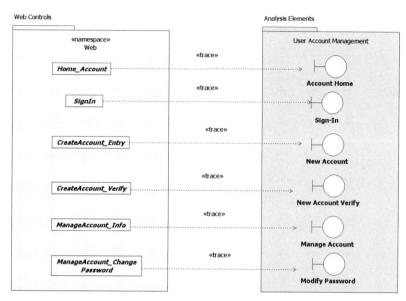

Figure 6-12: Tracing Web forms/controls to analysis classes.

identifies the connections between .NET Web control classes (.ascx.cs) and the dispatcher type of control classes.

Business Layer

Before addressing the dynamic part of the model, we should define the business layer of the Business packages. The detail of its structure is presented in Figure 6-14.

We have seen earlier in this chapter that the design model defines a logical organization of components into enterprise components, as it is presented in the business layer of Figure 6-14. The definition of this package is also a mechanical task, using as a reference the structure of the corresponding Use Case package in the analysis model. In the Control package of the analysis model you will find all the dispatcher type of control classes described (in the "Presentation Layer" section above), but also one entity manager control class (e.g., for User Account Management you will find the Account Management

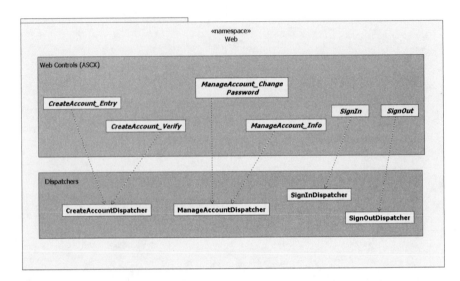

Figure 6-13: Participants in the presentation layer of User Account Management.

Figure 6-14: Structure detail of the Business Layer package.

control class). This situation is by virtue of the approach followed in the analysis model.

You thus define an enterprise component type of subsystem for that control class, as shown in Figure 6-14. Each enterprise component manages a subset of the entities defined in the key abstractions, and it is expressed with a specification and a realization, as represented in the structure of the package. The specification defines the interface that the enterprise component must support and the entities that it manages, thus giving an abstract specification of the behavior of the subsystem.

The interface defines everything a client needs to know in order to use the subsystem, acting as a contract of service definition with the client systems where it is integrated. This way an enterprise component can be replaced with a different implementation without any impact on the systems that integrate it. You can think of an interface as a specialization of a class defining only public operations. Note that an attribute is represented by its getter and setter operations. In Figure 6-14, the "lollipop" icon named "Account Manager" represents the interface, and this is the only type of design class that you will find in the Business package specification of the design model. As mentioned earlier, all other classes are defined in the implementation model and referenced in the design model.

The participants diagram of the specification package represents the enterprise component interface with the Data Layer classes that it manages, as depicted in Figure 6-15. Complementing the remark made earlier on the definitions of the Data Layer classes, the interface specification in this diagram represents the final result, as at this stage you are not yet in position to define the operations of the interface. For this you will also need to develop the sequence diagrams for all the use cases of the system.

As for any design element, the approach is not complete without a diagram to trace the design elements back to the analysis model, as represented in Figure 6-16. This diagram is located within the Business Layer package, as it is meant to represent the tracing for all the enterprise components of the Business package.

The second package of the enterprise component defines the realization of the interface, which models the interior of the subsystem the way that you will implement it. In other words, it is all that is not shown to any consumer of the service defined by the interface. To start off, usually a good guess is to define one class to correspond to the interface class. As usual, define the class with

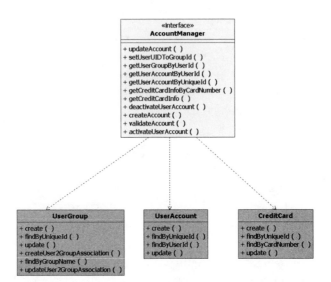

Figure 6-15: Enterprise component interface with associated Data Layer classes.

Microsoft Visual Studio .NET and then reverse engineer it in the implementation model. Then you can reference it in the design model, in the diagrams of the Realization package. In Figure 6-17 the "Traceability" diagram represents the implementation class in a realization relationship with its corresponding interface.

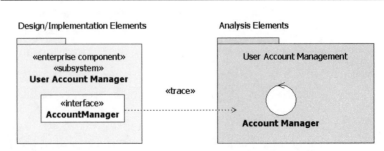

Figure 6-16: Tracing enterprise component interface to analysis classes.

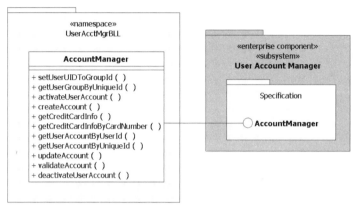

The AccountManager implementation class realizes
the specification of the AccountManager specification
as defined in the <<enterprise component>>
subsystem.

Figure 6-17: Realization of the enterprise component interface.

As for the interface definition, this is the final result. Note that the operations defined in the AccountManager implementation class are the same as in the AccountManager interface and will thus be defined at the same time during the development of the sequence diagrams.

The class diagram of Figure 6-18 shows all the classes that the enterprise component collaborates with. This diagram shows connections to and from other layers.

Use Case Realizations—Sequence Diagrams

The result of the activities so far is that you have defined a number of artifacts within the three following categories:

- In implementation you have created:
  - ❏ The code structure for all the classes that will be involved in the use case realization. These classes trace back to the classes identified in the key abstractions of the analysis model. Although it is always possible that you need new classes, with a well-designed analysis model, the

identified set of classes is likely to prove sufficient to support the system functions, as defined by the use cases.

❑ The database definition.

❑ The strongly typed DataSets and the XML Schema file that defines their structure, which also defines the class attributes. Thus you have completely specified the attributes of the entity classes of the analysis model.

❑ The Web forms and Web controls that represent the user experience model. As you have used the attributes of the screens and input forms of the user experience model, as well as their operations, you have also completely specified the boundary classes of the analysis model.

■ In the implementation model, you have imported the class definitions. As described earlier, a consequence of the approach in using the tools is that you need to have defined an implementation model structure as an initial step before starting with the design model activities. This step will be described in Chapter 7. Using a design tool like Rational XDE has the additional advantage of maintaining the consistency between the model

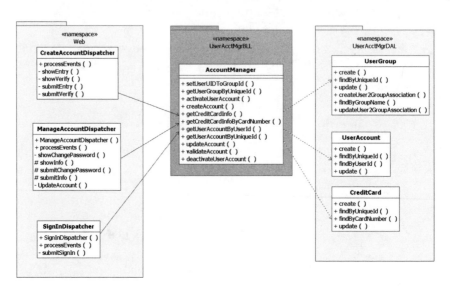

Figure 6-18: Class diagram for the enterprise component implementation.

and the code. This is an important enabler of the software engineering vision.

- In the design model, you have created the static part of the model:
  - ❏ The design model structure and class diagrams, with references to classes in the implementation model.
  - ❏ The interfaces of the enterprise components.
  - ❏ The database design model.

In reality, you also have defined the project structure in Microsoft Visual Studio .NET, as well as the structure of the implementation model. This needs to happen before starting the design model and is based on applying the approach defined in Chapter 7.

In order to complete the specification of the analysis classes into implementation classes, what is left is the definition of the operations of the entity and control classes (both dispatchers and entity managers). To define these operations you need to develop the dynamic part of the design model, which consists exclusively of designing sequence diagrams.

So far the activities of the design model were quite mechanical, with a lot of emphasis on defining a consistent and unified structure across the models. Defining a precise model structure along with the elements of the static part of the various models is aimed at helping the designers attain the correct mindset for the development of the sequence diagrams. Indeed, the critical design work will be done in the sequence diagrams, which are central in the modeling approach used:

- They permit identifying object responsibilities. These will be the object operations with their parameters and their attributes.
- They help to map class operations to use case scenarios and hence test cases.
- They are used to build the role-based security matrix by unveiling which objects and operations a specific actor (role) does access within the context of a specific use case.
- They are useful to verify that the classes are cohesive and comprehensive.

The sequence diagrams will sit within the use case realizations of a Business package, as presented in Figure 6-19.

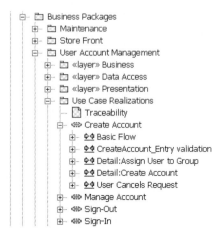

Figure 6-19: Structure detail of the Use Case Realizations package.

In this package, the "Traceability" diagram traces the use case realizations of the design model to the corresponding elements in the analysis model, as depicted in Figure 6-20.

At this stage of the process you work on a specific use case. Following the guiding principles introduced at the beginning of the chapter, your objective is to define sequence diagrams for all the use case scenarios identified in the analysis model, covering the basic flow of events but also all the alternate flows. In Figure 6-19 you can notice that for the Create Account use case the following sequence diagrams have been created: basic flow, CreateAccount_Entry validation (to present the interaction when some user data is invalid), and User Cancels Request. Two more diagrams are also created to present the details of some parts of the interaction in the basic flow diagram, thus avoiding cluttering the main sequence diagram: Detail:Create Account and Detail:Assign User to Group.

To create the sequence diagrams, you start off with the basic flow of the use case and consider the corresponding sequence diagram in the analysis model. In the design model you create a new sequence diagram and represent all the implementation classes that correspond to the analysis classes found in the analysis model sequence diagram. Because of the approach followed, initially the set of the classes will map one-to-one to the analysis classes. If in

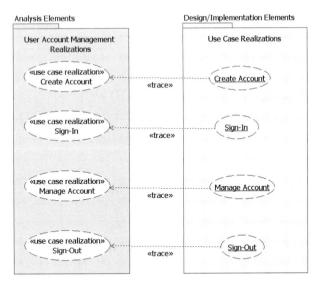

Figure 6-20: Tracing use case realizations from design to analysis.

doubt, the various traceability diagrams of the design model will help you find the correct implementation classes to use.

At this stage, the implementation classes have very few operations defined. You then review the messages in the analysis model, one at a time starting from the first message in the sequence, and try to find a corresponding operation in the implementation classes representing the recipients of the messages. As seen earlier, some classes like the code-behind classes will already have some operations defined. If you cannot find a corresponding operation, define a new operation in the code of the class and reverse engineer its definition before using it in the design diagram.

All messages that a class sends in response to one message received are part of the same operation, which represents its acting upon the received message. Thus, in the calling operation of the sender class, you can start writing code to represent the invocation of the operation on the recipient class. When defining an operation in the code, you should also apply a documentation strategy to describe the parameters of the operation and its purpose. Figure 6-21 presents an example of such a documentation structure. This approach

```
/// <summary>
/// createAccount: Adds the data in the UserInfo typed data set to the UserAccount table. Also
/// adds the data in the CreditCardInfo typed data set to the CreditCard table.
/// </summary>
/// <param name="dsUser">Typed data set UserInfo that contains the data to add.</param>
/// <param name="dsCreditCard">Typed data set CreditCardInfo that contains the data to add.</param>
/// <returns>Number of records that were added: 1 indicates 1 UserAccount record
/// was added, 2 indicates 1 UserAccount record and 1 CreditCard record
/// was added, 0 indicates no records were added.
/// The createAccount method updates the uniqueId field of dsUser and dsCreditCard
```

Figure 6-21: Documentation structure for a class method.

defines another level of system documentation, and some tools like Rational XDE define a mechanism to represent and synchronize this information as part of the model documentation.

Creating this kind of documentation while you develop the sequence diagrams also helps you better understand the purpose of each operation that you identify, thus effectively achieving the following objectives:

- Working toward producing a more cohesive design, as defined in the beginning of this chapter.

- Having a powerful consistency check between the sequence diagrams and the operation definitions. This activity cannot be automated, and consequently, if you think it is an important step, you should impose a discipline of executing consistency check reviews on the project.

- Optionally serving as the basis of the definition of an activity diagram to be attached to the operation definition in the implementation model, and describing its sequence of actions, as presented in a simple example in Figure 6-22. This is particularly useful for complex operations with many branches involved.

- As an additional advantage, it also serves the purpose of having code documentation from the early stages of coding.

The above description of the activities involved in the design of sequence diagrams defines an interactive approach to development, involving coding at

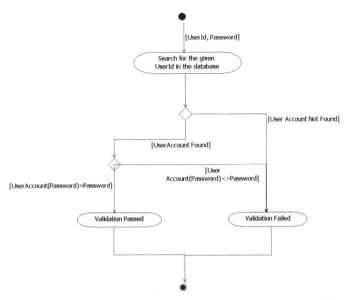

Figure 6-22: Activity graph: ValidateAccount in AccountManager class.

the same time as designing. This is a practical approach in designing these diagrams and has the following two advantages:

- It addresses the guiding principle that the design is defined in all detail, completely specifying the sequence diagrams by using only actual operation calls of the implementation classes.
- It defines a basis to maintain the consistency between the code and the design. In this perspective, the sequence diagrams have the responsibility to glue the design with the code, helping to trace back the code to the design.

You can apply this approach in two different ways, depending on how you divide the responsibilities between the people of your development team:

- Create only the operation definitions in the code, and possibly some limited code in order to call these operations from within the caller operations. This could be the situation when a designer is in charge of creating the initial skeleton of the application.

■ "Design While-U-Code," where the developers try to write as much code as they can imagine within the operations they identify. They also have the responsibility of developing the sequence diagrams for what they code. In that case you must distribute the work to individuals based on use cases. But because the classes are used for more than one use case, you will need to consolidate the operations defined by the various developers. Because what you give to the developers is indeed the coarsely defined sequence diagrams of the analysis model, you effectively implement an approach of not designing too much, while keeping the advantages of having a detailed design of the implementation, as described previously, especially the advantages related to sequence diagrams.

You can review in Figure 6-23 an example of a sequence diagram presenting the end result of this activity.

Design Mechanisms

An important objective of the design model is also to document the architecturally significant design mechanisms, as they have a broad impact on the system. This is an activity that should start early in system development, even while you create the use case model before the first iteration, and then should continue throughout the project lifetime. The objectives are to document the areas of the design bearing the highest technical risk or which are the most complex to comprehend. In this part of the design you are most likely to use design classes as well as models of the .NET technological framework.

In the overall design model structure, the design mechanisms will be lodged under the Common Elements package, as presented in Figure 6-24, in order to differentiate their models from the enterprise components and use case realizations. While it is important for the overall model consistency to make each design mechanism into its own package, the internal structure of the package should follow principles of practical judgment. You may use any combination of class, activity, and sequence diagrams that you deem the most appropriate to convey the explanation of these mechanisms. One of these complex technical areas is the role-based security mechanism, and its design model will be reviewed in the subsequent Case Study section.

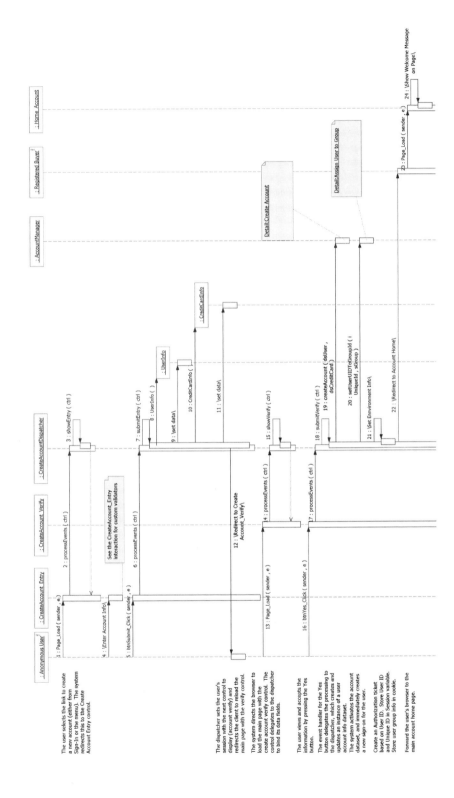

Figure 6-23: Sequence diagram for the basic flow of Create Account use case.

147

External Systems Adapters

In the analysis model we have discussed the use of adapters, represented as boundary classes. In the design model you have the following three choices for representing an adapter:

- The external system does not exhibit a .NET interface *or* you need to implement role-based security access to the external system. Create a design interface and an implementation class to realize it, then selectively define in the interface the subset of the external system operations (or API calls) that are used within your system. These operations will delegate their execution to the external system. This interface and corresponding implementation class effectively realizes the boundary component of the analysis model. Represent the external system interface in the sequence diagrams of your design model. This is the approach demonstrated in the present case study.

- The external system exhibits a .NET interface *and* you are not concerned about implementing role-based security access to the external system. Do not represent the external system at all, and consider that it is an implementation issue. You can consider the external system as an extension to the .NET framework, and in this case the guiding principles prevent you from representing its classes in collaborations of your design model. Instead, the collaboration with the external system will be represented as code, within an implementation class operation in your system. Note that there will still be some indirect role-based security access to the external system, defined by the role-based security access to the upstream classes that call on the external system.

- If, in either of the previous cases, the external system provides design- and implementation-level UML models, integrate them in the design model of your system. The boundary class of the analysis model will then be realized by some combination of classes in these models. For the time being, this is wishful thinking, as I have seen no package that provides you with this level of integration. You will also find a discussion on this topic in Appendix A.

The adapters to external systems are defined in the Common Elements package, as illustrated in Figure 6-24 with the Credit Card System adapter. The adapters are defined as subsystems stereotyped as enterprise components,

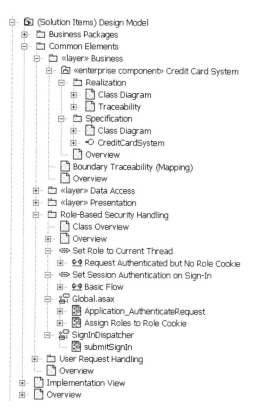

Figure 6-24: Structure detail of the Common package.

as the structure used for their specification is the same. The rationale behind this approach is that an adapter represents an enterprise component, which happens to be outside the scope of the current system.

Case Study

Continuing the development of the case study, we will apply the selected approach to the definition of the design model of the Create Account use case. But, because of the importance of capturing the design mechanism, we will also review the activity of documenting the role-based security design mechanism. Thus, this chapter will cover more than just the Create Account use case.

The design model of the Create Account use case is really defined by the sequence diagrams that cover all its flows of events, within use case scenarios. The sequence diagrams define the dynamic part of the model and rely on the existence of a definition of the static part. In the design model, as presented in the Approach, the static part consists of developing the class diagrams for all the classes that are involved in a Business package and is structured around the definition of the Data Access, Presentation, and Business layers.

Data Access Layer

In defining the Data Access Layer the starting point is the entity diagram of the analysis model presented in Figure 6-3. Applying the four-step process described in the Approach section, the first step has as an objective to produce the database design model presented in Figure 6-6.

First you create a one-to-one mapping of classes to tables. But you need to add an association table to support the many-to-many relationships between UserAccount and UserGroup. You define the table columns by reviewing the entity definitions in the glossaries. You also define for each table an identifying column as the primary key. Then you map the relationships defined in the analysis model of Figure 6-3, using the identity columns as foreign keys. Define all the constraints you need and complete this step with the generation of the database definition in the RDBMS.

After creating the database design model, use Microsoft Visual Studio .NET for the second step (that is, the creation of the XML Schema files). Connect to the database with the Server Explorer and create a new item of type XML Schema (e.g., CreditCardInfo.xsd for the CreditCard table), opening it in its designer. Then drag and drop one of the tables on the designer (e.g., the CreditCard table), update the XML definition to reflect the naming you want to apply for the class, and associate "MSDataSetGenerator" to the "Custom Tool" property of the file.

In the third step, you select the file in the project and apply the "Run Custom Tool" action, which will generate a C# code file (.cs) with the same name as the corresponding XML Schema file (.xsd) (e.g., CreditCardInfo.cs).

In the fourth and final step, use the reverse-engineering feature of the design tool to reverse engineer the C# code file into the implementation model. You now have the strongly typed DataSets representing the Data Type classes, named after the table names (e.g., CreditCardInfo).

You then proceed by defining the Data Access Layer classes in Microsoft Visual Studio .NET. The relevant classes are named UserGroup, UserAccount, and CreditCard. We defining the following operations:

- The create operation; e.g., "public int create(CreditCardInfo dsCredit-Card)."
- The retrieve by primary key operation; e.g., "public CreditCardInfo find-ByUniqueId (long uniqueId)."
- The update operation; e.g., "public int update(CreditCardInfo dsCredit-Card)."

In the case study we do not have a delete operation, as a CreditCard can only be deleted when its parent UserAccount is also deleted. Due to the concise nature of the case study, this does not happen either, as, in the Maintenance Business package, we only deactivate an account, we do not physically delete it from the database. Nevertheless, because of the referential integrity constraint defined on the relationship, there is no need to provision any operation for deleting a CreditCard, as the RDBMS will handle this operation whenever the corresponding UserAccount is deleted.

To complete this activity you also need to reverse engineer the Data Layer class definitions in the implementation model. Then you are in the position to create the Data Access Layer diagram of Figure 6-4, and the trace diagram of Figure 6-7, thus effectively completing the definition of the Data Access Layer package.

Presentation Layer

Following the process described in the Approach, you will first identify the dispatcher classes from the analysis model and create their code definition with Microsoft Visual Studio .NET, without defining any operations, as these are to be unveiled with the sequence diagrams. Then, you reverse engineer the definitions in the implementation model and are able to create the trace diagram presented earlier in Figure 6-11.

Next, you will make a more extensive use of Microsoft Visual Studio .NET to create the Web forms or controls. The presentation mechanism of the case study sample is based on using Web controls that are loaded within a single container Web form. You can review the design code and mechanism by downloading the sample from www.BooksREasy.com. I will not delve into the details of this mechanism, as it does not add much to the current discussion. It is sufficient to say that all the screens and input forms modeled in the user experience model will translate into Web controls. As for the Web form mentioned previously, it is represented only in the design mechanism model and not in any of the models representing the business functionality.

Note that the overall navigability of the site is defined within this design mechanism, being attached to the site's header file. Although the navigability depends on the state achieved by the outcome of a use case, I have chosen not to model this collaboration in the subsequent sequence diagrams. You have to exercise practical judgment in deciding how much you model of a system, as there is always a point where the additional effort brings only marginal value. As a good practice, you should, at the least, model the business functionality in all details.

You create one Web control (.ascx) for each boundary class in the analysis model. Using the boundary traceability diagram of the analysis model, you can trace back the boundary class to the user experience screen and input form of the user experience model. Using the information found in this model you are able to design the Web control in Microsoft Visual Studio .NET, which will also generate the code-behind class in the corresponding file (.ascx.cs). The screen attributes and input form fields will turn into input fields, and the screen operations into commands and navigations. Then you are able reverse engineer the code-behind classes into the implementation model and produce the Web control trace diagram of Figure 6-12, and the presentation layer participants diagram of Figure 6-13. Note that the implementation model of the code-behind classes defines most of the operations of these classes, as these operations are generated by Microsoft Visual Studio .NET.

Business Layer

As seen earlier, the Business package of User Account Management defines one enterprise component, namely User Account Manager. Applying the described approach, you first define the specification, where you define a design class to represent the component interface. This is the only type of design class you are likely to define in this part of the design, as you use references to implementation classes within your design model diagrams. Figure 6-15 presents the component interface with its managed entities, while Figure 6-16 presents the traceability of the interface to the corresponding control class in the analysis model.

In the realization of the enterprise component you should define an AccountManager class within Microsoft Visual Studio .NET and reverse engineer it in the implementation model. Operations are to be defined later using the sequence diagrams. The defined implementation class realizes the enterprise component interface as presented in Figure 6-17. Finally, create the participants diagram of Figure 6-18, where you represent all classes related to the realization of the enterprise component.

Use Case Realizations—Sequence Diagrams

Having addressed the static part of the design model, you can move to the dynamic part where the critical work of unveiling the class operations will take place. This will be based on the development of the sequence diagrams for the Create Account use case.

As a first step, define the trace diagram for the use case realization, as depicted in Figure 6-20.

Then, using the corresponding sequence diagrams of the analysis model, and following the approach described, you will interactively create the code and develop the sequence diagrams for the design model. The end result was presented earlier in Figure 6-23. Notice how this diagram represents the action of signing in to the newly created user account and navigating to the Home_Account page. We could have directly represented the navigation with a Page_Load message from the CreateAccountDispatcher to the Home_Account page. This was not done for two reasons:

- The reality of the interaction is a bit more complex and is represented by a design mechanism named the User Request Handling. It would be of no value to represent that interaction.
- The objective of presenting it like this is to clearly represent in the design that there is a change in the nature of the role involved in the completion of the interaction. It is important to represent this change, to facilitate the development of the role-based security model (this will be explained in Chapter 8).

Conceptually we can also understand this interaction as presenting a message that sources upstream of the Registered Buyer class—that is, from the CreateAccountDispatcher class.

In the detail design you ought to represent the interaction in every detail. Thus, to avoid the cluttering of the main sequence diagram, you can reference within the diagram other sequence diagrams presenting some details of the collaborations. Figure 6-25 presents the detail of the validation of the Web control, when the user submits the data to the Web server.

Figures 6-26 and 6-27 present two additional significant details of the collaboration.

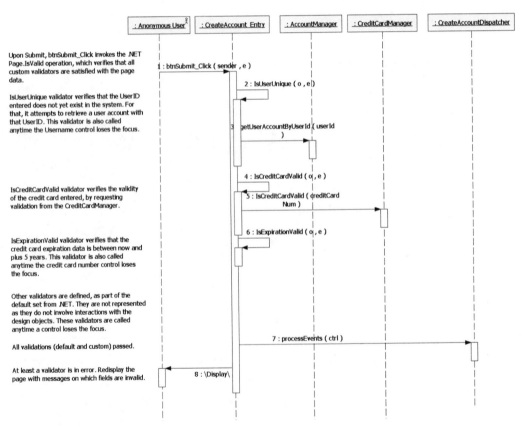

Figure 6-25: Collaboration detail: CreateAccount_Entry validation.

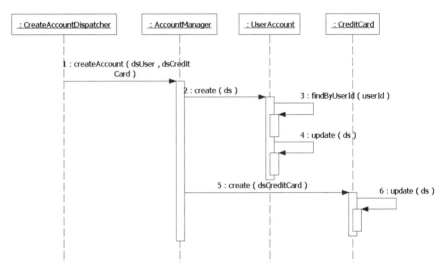

Figure 6-26: Collaboration detail: Create Account.

While developing the sequence diagrams and unveiling class operations, it is sometimes useful to also attach an activity diagram to some operations, especially for the more complex ones. The activity diagrams are also useful to help

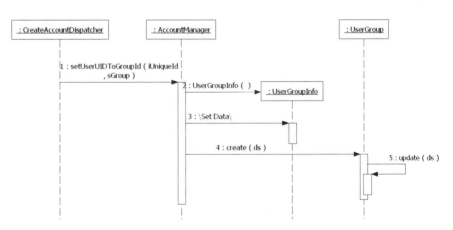

Figure 6-27: Collaboration detail: Adding User to Group.

achieve class coherence as well as validate the consistency of the sequence diagrams. At the same time you should exercise practical judgment in order to avoid going overboard with defining activity diagrams. An example of such a diagram was presented in Figure 6-22 for the ValidateAccount operation of the AccountManager class (documented in Figure 6-17).

Design Mechanism: Role-Based Security Handling

As an example of documenting a design mechanism, this section will review role-based security handling. In documenting a design mechanism, you have to use any combination of diagrams that you deem appropriate to convey a detailed and comprehensive understanding of the mechanism. This will usually include some class, sequence, and activity diagrams.

The role-based security mechanism has two aspects:

■ The Sign-In mechanism, to ensure that after a user has successfully signed in, all browser requests within the current session are authenticated.

■ The Web page request authentication mechanism. When a page request arrives for a session, and if you have activated some form of authentication in Web.config, .NET generates an application event to give the opportunity to the application to apply its own processing for the request authentication.

Figure 6-28 shows the class diagram for both aspects of the mechanism. The right side presents the classes involved in the sign-in mechanism—that is, the SignInDispatcher and the SignIn Web control, presented by its code-behind class.

The left side of the figure presents the classes involved in the Web page request authentication mechanism, which is only the Global class, defined in Global.asax.

In the middle of the figure are classes that both mechanisms collaborate with. Association relationships are used for classes that are instantiated by the SignInDisptacher and Global classes. The references to the instantiated objects are maintained in the application. Dependency relationships are used for classes that provide some service, without needing to instantiate a specific instance. Static members of .NET classes define these services.

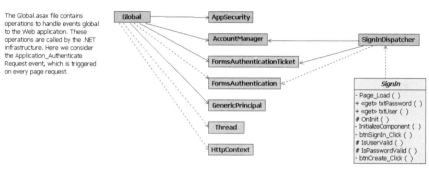

The Global.asax file contains operations to handle events global to the Web application. These operations are called by the .NET infrastructure. Here we consider the Application_Authenticate Request event, which is triggered on every page request.

When signing in, two things need to happen: 1) Set session variables to hold the UserID so that the User Request Handling mechanism can operate. 2) Set a session authentication ticket so that the Role-Based Security Handling mechanism can operate.

The mechanism operates by: 1) setting a session authentication ticket with the UserID, so that when the Application_Authenticate event is called, it is possible to retrieve it from the session call context, and thus reference the corresponding user account.

2) Saving the groups that the user participates in the role cookie, so that it is also possible to access them when the Application_ Authenticate event is called.

3) Creating a new GenericPrincipal with the roles in the cookie and assign the principal to the current thread and context.

4) The .NET infrastructure is responsible for verifying that for each operation called, the current thread principal contains a role listed in the ones that are authorized for that operation.

Figure 6-28: Role-based security handling: Participants.

When the user submits the SignIn form, the form delegates the processing to the SignInDispatcher. This is a general pattern in the sample application and is defined by another design mechanism. The SignInDispatcher determines the system state and delegates the processing to its submitSignIn operation. The activity graph in Figure 6-29 explains the sequence of actions to achieve an authenticated browser session, based on attaching an authentication cookie to the session. At the same time, an authentication ticket is created and attached to a cookie, with the roles that the current user assumes.

Figure 6-30 presents the class collaborations that correspond to the SignIn use case. Note that these collaborations might not be represented the same way in the use case realization of the corresponding Business package, as the concerns are different. In this diagram you focus on presenting the collaboration with the .NET architecture classes, whereas in a Business package realization you focus on the system classes only.

When a user has successfully signed in, every page request from the current browser session will have an authentication cookie attached.

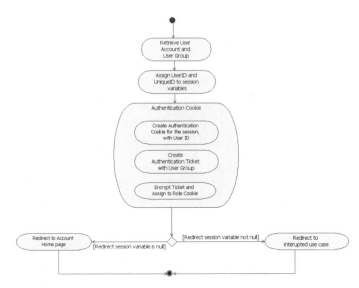

Figure 6-29: Activity graph: submitSignIn in SignInDispatcher class.

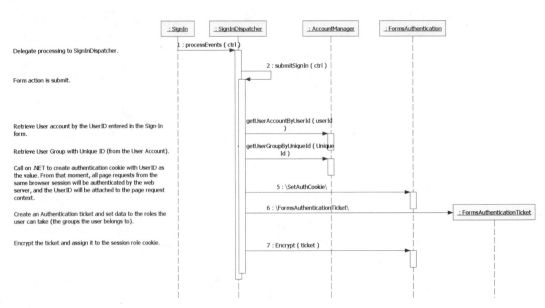

Figure 6-30: Sequence diagram: Set Session Authentication on Sign-In.

```
<authentication mode="Forms">
    <forms name=".ASPXAUTHBOOKSREASY" protection="All" timeout="60" />
</authentication>
```

Figure 6-31: Declare forms authentication in Web.config.

If you have specified some form of authentication in Web.config (e.g., forms authentication as depicted in Figure 6-31), and if you have implemented the Application_AuthenticateRequest in the Global.asax, the .NET framework will generate a call to this operation as the first event of every Web page request.

The activity graph of Figure 6-32 presents the sequence of actions of this operation.

Finally, the sequence diagram of Figure 6-33 improves the understanding of the mechanism, by describing the collaboration in a scenario where the cookie containing the user roles is not attached to the session. This is different

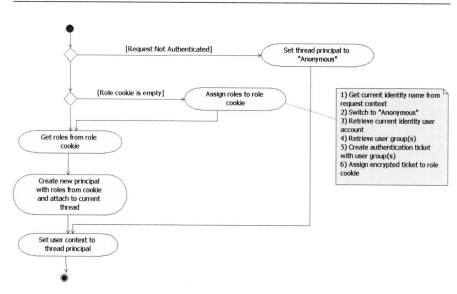

Figure 6-32: Activity graph: Application_AuthenticateRequest in Global class.

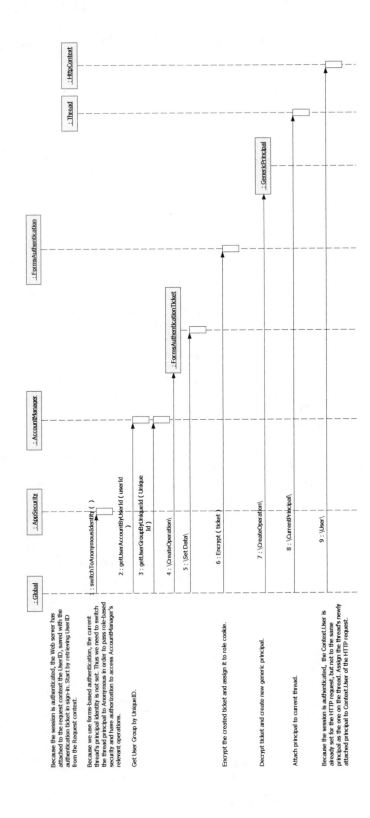

Figure 6-33: Sequence diagram: Request authenticated but no role cookie.

from the authentication cookie, which is always present for an authenticated browser session.

In the sequence diagram you can notice the switchToAnonymousIdentity operation of the AppSecurity class. The name of the operation is self-explanatory, and Figure 6-34 presents its definition.

In this definition you can notice that the class has an attribute adornment of SecurityPermissionAttribute, which specifies a demand for the code of this class to be executed only if at least one caller on the call stack has a permission to control the current principal (ControlPrincipal=true). Indeed, changing the security principal is a privileged operation, and you want to prevent any form of malicious usage of the system by some code that would be able to change its role and assume a more privileged role, gaining access to system functions that are not within its normal reach.

This type of security check is defined as an evidence-based or code-based type of security and is controlled by the Runtime Security Policy of the .NET Framework Configuration. A complete discussion on the configuration of code-based security is beyond the scope of this book. You can find more information on the related concepts in the .NET framework SDK documentation, which comes with the .NET framework. For the purpose of the current discussion, it is sufficient to say that you need to select or define a code group

```
/// <summary>
/// General class for application security functions
/// </summary>
[SecurityPermissionAttribute(SecurityAction.Demand, ControlPrincipal =true)]
public class AppSecurity
{
    /// <summary>
    /// Switch the identity of the current thread to Anonymous
    /// </summary>
    public static void switchToAnonymousIdentity()
    {
        //Create new Generic Identity
        GenericIdentity currUser = new GenericIdentity("Anonymous");
        //Create new generic Principal and assign roles user is playing
        string[] rolesArray={"Anonymous"};
        Generic Principal currPrincipal = new GenericPrincipal (currUser,rolesArray );

        //Attach the principal to the current thread.
        Thread.CurrentPrincipal = currPrincipal;
    }
}
```

Figure 6-34: Operation definition: switchToAnonymousIdentity.

that references every assembly that is likely to call the operation switch-ToAnonymousIdentity. Obviously, the selected code group should reference only trusted assemblies (e.g., the application you are developing for your organization). Then, select or define a Permission Set to attach to the code group, making sure that the Security permission enables the "Allow principal control" permission.

Summary

In this chapter we reviewed the activities related to the development of the design model. The principal input artifact for this activity is the analysis model. The user experience model is also used in order to specify the attributes, input fields, and navigation items of the Web forms or controls. Finally, the glossaries are used to define the columns of the tables in the database model. A practical approach for developing the design model is to develop it in parallel with the code structure using Microsoft Visual Studio .NET. A preliminary step is to also define the implementation model. Very few classes are defined in the design model, because all the diagrams reference the classes of the implementation model, which needs to be maintained consistent with the code. Ideally, the consistency is achieved by using an automatic synchronization feature of the design tool.

The steps involved in the design model are

- Create the model structure.
- Define the UML database design model and create or generate the database. Use the XML Schema feature of .NET to generate strongly typed DataSets.
- Define the presentation layer, by creating the Web forms or controls with Microsoft Visual Studio .NET and modeling only the code-behind classes.
- Define the business layer around the concept of enterprise components, with an interface specification.

■ Create sequence diagrams for all the flows of events of the use cases. This is a very important activity, as it will unveil the class operations, as well as create the definitions in code. A practical approach is to design it in parallel with coding the class collaborations.

An important objective of the design model is also to document the architecturally significant design mechanisms, which define the areas of the design bearing the highest technical risk or that are the most complex to comprehend.

The design model also defines the detail specification of the various adapters for the external systems, represented with boundary classes in the analysis model.

At the end of the design model you transition into the coding or implementation phase. Even while coding, you should use all the capabilities of your tools, as well as the techniques and processes to continually maintain the consistency of the code with the model. This is how you will be able to implement traceability, which is the central concept of the software engineering approach promoted in this book.

Chapter 7

Implementation Model

Introduction

The implementation model deals with concepts that represent the physical elements of files and directories on a computer system. In a simple definition, the implementation model is purely a static model, representing the system classes organized in files, within directory hierarchies, with their dependencies.

This chapter is not aimed at covering all the issues related to the representation and management of implementation elements, but instead addresses the practical issue of organizing the code files and representing their dependencies. The code files contain the definitions of the implementation classes, and the file structure will drive the definition of the .NET assemblies that will be produced. Hence, the identified dependencies impose a certain order in the development of the .NET assemblies composing the solution. Other issues like configuration management (releases, access control, etc.) will not be covered. Also, a complete implementation model should cater to the representation of all artifacts involved in the solution, including the model documentation, executable files, and test scripts.

The proposed approach is but one possible approach, as the choices made for the creation of the project structure and implementation model are not the most critical activities in the process. Nevertheless, this chapter presents a practical approach to structuring Microsoft Visual Studio .NET projects, in order to achieve consistency with the unified model structure used throughout the various models produced so far. The implementation model, in turn, stems from the structure of the files and directories within the project. As a consequence, the resulting approach is totally oriented towards a .NET development environment.

Approach

In the previous chapter, the approach presented mandates the creation of an implementation model before starting the design model. The reality is that you can create the structure of the design model without having to reference the implementation model, because the implementation model is useful only when referencing implementation classes in the various diagrams of the design model. Creating the structure of the design model is a prerequisite, as this structure will be the starting point to define the project structure in Microsoft Visual Studio .NET.

In this chapter I will focus on presenting an approach applied to Microsoft Visual Studio .NET Enterprise Architect. This version, compared with the other versions, has the additional features of Enterprise Template Projects. For the case study I shall take advantage of the Enterprise Template Projects, which are equivalent to packages in UML models. Thus this feature is very convenient in helping you to structure your projects into packages. At the end of the discussion I will describe the result as it would appear in the other versions of Microsoft Visual Studio .NET.

Project Structure in Microsoft Visual Studio .NET

Having defined the structure of the design model, creating the project structure in Microsoft Visual Studio .NET is very much a mechanical task of mapping the packages of the design model by applying some very simple rules. In order to support the discussion, Figure 7-1 presents the resulting project structure in parallel with the design model structure.

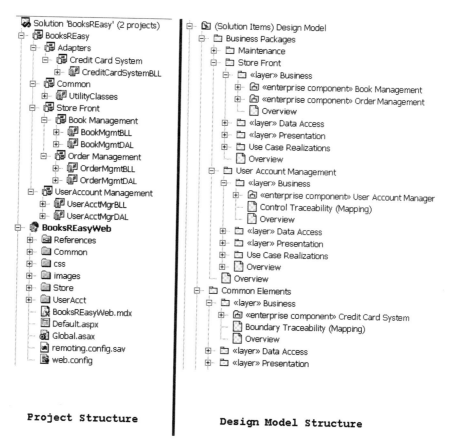

Figure 7-1: Project structure versus design model structure.

You can notice in the figure that the focus of the design model structure is on the enterprise components. For each Business package, create one Enterprise Template Project (e.g., Store Front in Figure 7-1). For each enterprise component in a Business package, create an Enterprise Template Project under the corresponding Business package (e.g., Order Management in Store Front). In Figure 7-1 you can notice that because User Account Management is the only enterprise component in its Business package, a shortcut has been taken and only one level of Enterprise Template Project created.

You can also notice that the Maintenance Business package does not appear, as it has not been implemented. The assumption is that this package is not in the scope of the current iteration and it should not be specified in use cases. Thus it should not appear either in the analysis model or subsequent design and implementation models (it does appear in the analysis and design models for the sake of avoiding any confusion while presenting the model structure, at the corresponding stage of the discussion).

In the design model, the external systems adapters were defined, under the Common Elements package, as subsystems stereotyped as enterprise components. To keep this distinctive treatment in the project structure, you define a general Enterprise Template Project named Adapters. For each Adapter package defined in the design model, create an Enterprise Template Project named after the adapter (e.g., Credit Card System).

Next, for each Enterprise Template Project, create two class library projects, one for the Business Layer and one for the Data Access Layer, in order to mirror the two corresponding layer packages found in the Business Component packages of the design model. As a convention, the Business Layer project has a suffix of BLL and the Data Access Layer has a suffix of DAL. In this case study we create C# class library projects. The overall idea is to assign the implementation classes that are defined within a layer of the design model, to the corresponding project in the project structure. Note that for the Credit Card System Enterprise Template Project we do not define a Data Access Layer project, as this subsystem does not involve any class persistence.

In Figure 7-1 you can notice one additional Enterprise Template Project named Common, containing one project named Utility Classes. This project will contain all files and implementation classes that are of general use. In particular you will find in this project the definitions of the Data Type classes, which are potentially used by all classes (as explained in Chapter 6). The definitions of these classes appear in the project as XML Schema files (.xsd). These files are associated with the MSDataSetGenerator tool. When building the solution, Microsoft Visual Studio .NET ensures that the strongly typed DataSets are generated by this tool and then compiles and builds the generated files into an assembly.

Thus the traceability of the C# DataSet definition files to the xsd files is managed automatically by Microsoft Visual Studio .NET. This is important to understand in the perspective of the software engineering vision of Chapter 1, as you must always ask yourself how one artifact traces back to the specifications, and tools are one of the ways to implement traceability. Other types of class definitions to include in this project are any type of library class (e.g., the AppSecurity implementation class mentioned in the role-based security handling mechanism in Chapter 6).

The presentation layers of the Business packages are treated somehow differently. As the target system is a Web site, the Web forms and all files involved in presentation logic will be defined within a virtual directory on a Web server. For this reason, all the presentation layers of all Business packages will be created within one project, as presented in Figure 7-1, where the Web project is named BooksREasyWeb and its type is ASP.NET Web Application.

Note that creating this kind of project in Microsoft Visual Studio .NET will also ensure that the corresponding virtual directory is defined in the Web server. Figure 7-2 presents the significant details of the BooksREasyWeb

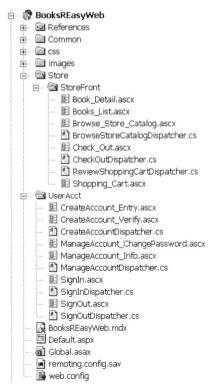

Figure 7-2: Structure of an ASP.NET Web Application project.

project. In the project structure you can notice the organization of the Web forms and control files according to the Business package they correspond to. The Common directory holds mainly Web forms and controls involved in the Common mechanism mentioned in Chapter 6.

As a result of applying the previous steps, you have defined a number of projects in the Microsoft Visual Studio .NET solution, as presented in Figure 7-1. As a matter of verification, here is the list of these projects: Credit-CardSystemBLL, UtilityClasses, BookMgmtBLL, BookMgmtDAL, Order-MgmtBLL, OrderMgmtDAL, UserAcctMgmtBLL, UserAcctMgmtDAL, and BooksREasyWeb.

At the same time, you have to define for each of the projects created the assembly name and the default namespace that will be used for the classes created in the project. The convention used in this case study for both of these elements is to compose the name on the basis of the logical path defined by the project structure, adding a standard prefix of "BooksREasy" (e.g., for the Credit Card System: BooksREasy.Adapters.CreditCardSystem.CreditCardSystemBLL).

One exception is for the BooksREasyWeb project, as this project integrates the presentation layers of all the Business packages. The assembly and default namespace are named BooksREasy.Web.

Having defined the project structure, you will start creating code files (.cs) to hold the definitions of the implementation classes that you identify during design. Organizing the implementation classes into files is very much a matter of style and practicality, while you should consider the impact of your choices on the maintainability of the code. Thus, choosing to put the definition of two or more classes within one code file will mainly depend on how much you consider these classes to be related.

To complete this section, it is interesting to consider what happens when using other versions of Microsoft Visual Studio .NET. In the above approach, only the Enterprise Template Project feature of Microsoft Visual Studio .NET Enterprise Architect was used. When using other versions you will still create the same list of projects, the only difference being that you will not be able to structure the projects into a hierarchy.

Implementation Model Structure

The next activity is to create an implementation model in UML. With this model you have three objectives:

- Present the directory and file structure of the physical artifacts (code files and other files) that compose the Microsoft Visual Studio .NET projects in your solution.

- Present the namespace structure of your .NET solution. Documenting this aspect of the knowledge for the components you are developing for the current system will facilitate their subsequent integration and reuse in other solutions.

- Present the dependencies of the components, more specifically the dependencies of the .NET assemblies produced by the solution. These dependencies will be presented in the implementation view of the solution.

The implementation model is structured around the two concepts of .NET assemblies and namespaces. In the previous section we defined a number of projects that will produce corresponding .NET assemblies. Thus, it is a good practice to define one implementation model per project in the solution structure. A practical consequence of this approach is that when you have to define a class in code as a result of the design activity, you reverse engineer it in the corresponding implementation model. Within each implementation model, the model structure defines two views, as presented in Figure 7-3:

- One view presents the file structure of your .NET solution, the physical artifacts, which are presented by components stereotyped as files.

- The other view presents the .NET namespaces, presented by packages stereotyped as namespaces.

This model structure addresses the first two objectives of the implementation model as stated earlier.

The physical artifact view is contained within the Artifacts package, which is distinctively stereotyped as "fileArtifacts." This view mirrors the hierarchy of directories and files defining the project. Note the convention to represent a code-behind file (e.g., Default.aspx.cs in Figure 7-3), as part of the corresponding Web class file. File directories are presented as packages stereotyped as "directory," while files are presented as components stereotyped as "file."

The namespace view is presented as a hierarchy of packages all stereotyped as "namespace," with the hierarchy matching the namespace definition (for example, for the namespace "BooksREasy.Web," defined in the project

Figure 7-3: Structure of the implementation model.

BooksREasyWeb, there are two nested namespace packages, as depicted in Figure 7-3). All classes are defined within the terminal package of the corresponding namespace. You could also have two namespace definitions within one code file. In that situation you have more than one branch of namespace packages in the implementation model, as presented in Figure 7-4.

The elements of these two views are related by a reside relationship (defined in UML) to indicate that a class resides in a component, as presented in the partial diagram of Figure 7-5. Some file components do not define implementation classes and will thus have no relationships defined (e.g., image files).

Figure 7-4: Multiple namespaces defined within one code file.

Note that by definition of this type of relationship in UML, the direction of the relationship is from the component to the class, to express that the class is the supplier and the component is the consumer. Thus a component can have relationships with multiple classes.

The implementation classes in the model should be accurate representations of the corresponding code. This was expressed in Chapter 6 by the assumption that the design tool has a comprehensive set of capabilities to represent the semantics of the underlying technology. The .NET framework has simplified the job of tool vendors in this perspective, as it defines a unique set of semantics for all coding languages. This is achieved by the constraint imposed on all .NET languages to support the Common Language Specification (CLS), which defines these semantics. The term "semantics" used in the context of .NET refers to the list of concepts that are supported by the CLS (e.g., abstract classes, sealed classes, static members, delegates, and all other CLS concepts). Rational XDE for .NET is an example of a tool supporting the CLS semantics.

Figure 7-5: Files and classes in a reside relationship.

Implementation View

So far we have addressed the first two objectives of the implementation model, as defined at the beginning of the previous section. The third objective of presenting the dependencies between the assemblies is achieved by creating the implementation view. This is a diagram that is best created in the design model, as it presents an overall view of all the implementation models, and because of the reliance of the design activities on the implementation models. Figure 7-6 presents the implementation view.

An important point to comprehend is that the dependencies expressed in this diagram map exactly to the dependencies defined within the Project Dependencies feature of Microsoft Visual Studio .NET. This is another example of tracing of the knowledge, in this case between some project configuration information maintained by Microsoft Visual Studio .NET and the implementation model.

Case Study

For the implementation model it is not possible to apply the approach by focusing only on the Create Account use case. The objective of the designer is not to create only what is sufficient for a specific use case; this is impossible to know when developing the initial project structure and implementation models, which in turn is a prerequisite to developing the design model. For this reason, you should remember that all implementation classes and associated files presented in this chapter are defined later, after applying the process described in Chapter 6, and would not appear on the initial project structure and implementation models. The designer applies the approach focusing on what is in the design model structure, created as the first step of the design model. In doing so here are the resulting artifacts:

- Figure 7-1 presents the project structure.
- Figure 7-2 presents the details of the Web project after the design model is completed. When creating the initial implementation model and project structure, only the directory structure can be imagined.
- The same remark applies for the implementation model of Figure 7-3.

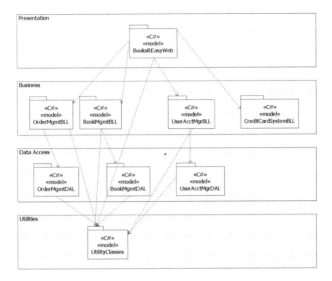

Figure 7-6: Implementation view.

- The implementation view of Figure 7-6 can only partially be defined in the initial stage of the implementation model. You can only represent the implementation models and their allocation to software layers. During the development of the design model you should complete this view with the dependencies that you will unveil.

After the design model is completed, the resulting implementation models will also have the implementation classes and the files containing them.

Summary

In this chapter we reviewed the activities related to the development of the implementation model. The principal input artifact for this activity is the structure of the design model, which is created as the first step in the design model. The enterprise components will map to Enterprise Template Project, each one subdivided into a business layer and data layer project. The presentation layer for all the Business packages will map into one Web project. Each project defines a number of files organized into directories.

The implementation model is defined by one model for each project created in the solution, and it also corresponds to the .NET assembly produced by the project. These models are structured along two views, the physical artifacts and the namespaces. The physical artifact view defines a hierarchy of packages stereotyped as "directory" containing components stereotyped as "file." The namespace view defines one or more hierarchies of packages stereotyped as "namespace." The leaf elements of the namespace hierarchy are the implementation classes. Files and implementation classes are related by reside relationships.

The implementation view is a diagram of the design model that defines the dependencies between the different models. Hence, it also defines the dependencies between .NET assemblies, as each implementation model corresponds to a .NET assembly.

Chapter 8

Role-Based Security

Introduction

In the interconnected world that we live in, more and more software systems are required to expose some of their functions as services accessible from the Internet. These services were until recently defined only as a Web interface, but with the advent of Web services it is clear that every element of a software system is potentially distributed over the Internet and accessible as other types of interfaces, particularly SOAP interfaces. In this context, security has become a major issue in software development.

We can define three major layers in system security:

- Physical infrastructure security, which deals with issues like network security, firewalls, and demilitarized network zones, and also with operating system, Web server, and database security configurations.

- Technology infrastructure security, also referred to as application server security, which deals with issues like role-based security and evidence-based security.

- Application security, which defines the design mechanisms that applications implement to control the access of the users to its various functions. This aspect of security deals with concerns like which buttons or menu items to show or hide to the user on any specific screen, depending on the user's identity. These design mechanisms may or may not rely on the role-based security of the technology infrastructure.

Because the overall focus of this book is on the specification of functional aspects of the system within a .NET context, presentation of physical infrastructure security is beyond the scope of this discussion.

Application security falls within the realm of design mechanisms. One such mechanism is the role-based security mechanism that was reviewed in Chapter 6, because it complements the discussion of design models. On the other hand, application security does not directly or necessarily relate to .NET considerations, but more to application patterns and frameworks. Consequently, a discussion of application security does not contribute extra value to the overall understanding of the concepts presented, and for the sake of conciseness will not be covered in this book. If you download the code and models for BooksREasy, you will be able to examine the application security design mechanism used for that application, which is based on defining a mapping between roles and use cases on the one hand, and use cases and screens on the other. This design mechanism defines a very useful pattern that can be reused in any application that has been engineered using a use case-driven approach.

For further reading on security:

- *Secrets and Lies: Digital Security in a Networked World* gives a thorough coverage of infrastructure security.
- Read *.NET Framework Security* for in-depth information on all aspects of .NET security.
- I refer you to *Building Secure Software: How to Avoid Security Problems the Right Way* on how to integrate security considerations in the broader software development lifecycle. In particular this book addresses coding techniques for security.

The discussion in this chapter will concentrate on the role-based security of .NET and how it integrates with the overall software engineering approach presented, demonstrating a way to implement traceability of the security configuration back to the system specification. A general discussion on evidence-based security is also beyond the scope of this book (only a short discussion in Chapter 6 has reviewed the specific implications of evidence-based security in relation to the role-based security design mechanism).

Although security is often perceived to be just a complex infrastructure issue, hence very peripheral to system specification and coding, it is interesting to note how a software engineering approach to software development has such an important impact on this major issue, addressing no less than two of the three levels of security: technology infrastructure (with role-based security) and application security (with design mechanism). As a consequence, the premise of using such an approach is to be able to define a standard setup and configuration of the physical infrastructure, and hence achieve a more robust, stable, and easily maintainable infrastructure.

As introduced in Chapter 6, one of the advantages of a mature technological platform like .NET is that it enables software systems to be implemented as applications running within the controlled environment of an application server. This control takes the form of a series of services, typically transaction monitoring, connection, thread and object pooling, queued components, loosely coupled events, and security. The overall thinking behind the use of a controlled environment is that application developers do not need to implement these mechanisms, as the application server will implement them better and more effectively. Thus, application developers are able to focus on the business logic of the application they develop, and leave the rest to the application server.

One of the mechanisms that "old type" applications would develop again and again is access control to the various functions of the system. Obviously, very few people are excited when asked to develop from scratch security mechanisms for their applications. Most experienced developers know how difficult and tricky this can be and would welcome any ready-made solution, like the role-based security that is implemented by an application server like .NET.

Every class in a .NET application has a series of publicly accessible operations. The principle of role-based security is that:

- Application developers identify roles that can access the objects. A role defines a category of actual users and is equivalent to an actor in the use case model.

- Each role is associated with a list of one or more actual users of the system. Conversely, an actual user can be associated to more than one role, reflecting the roles the user plays in the organization.

- Each class and each operation of the application is associated with a specific role.

This association of class operation with roles is achieved in .NET by usage of a specific set of .NET attributes. Thus, the developer implements the code of the class operations without any security considerations in mind, with the perspective that only one user will use the system. Role-based security configuration is implemented as a distinct activity of defining the appropriate role-based security attributes for the class operations. When the application is installed in the controlled environment of the .NET server, the .NET framework will monitor all the calls to the classes and their operations and enforce security access according to the configuration. The .NET framework has the responsibility to identify the actual user who is at the source of a particular call to an operation. The outcome of this identification depends solely on the configuration of the .NET role-based security.

All this seems nice and easy, but there is a very important decision process that has to take place:

- Decide which roles are adequate for the application.

- Decide which implementation classes and operations can be accessed by each role.

Unfortunately, these decisions can engender endless debate and slow down development. The approach presented in this chapter can help you avoid these obstacles by removing guesswork and systematizing the decision-making process. By cutting back on "freeform" decision areas, it can help developers not only improve the effectiveness of the process, but also achieve consistent quality throughout the application.

Approach

The proposed approach integrates within the overall software engineering approach presented in this book and addresses the role-based security model at two levels:

- In the analysis model it presents a coarse level of specification, focused on defining role-based security at the granularity of an analysis class.
- In the design model it defines in detail the .NET role-based security configuration to be applied to every implementation class and operation.

Both levels of specification refer to the actor model in the use case model. Also, both levels of specification rely on the sequence diagrams of the corresponding analysis or design models. This is another demonstration of the importance of sequence diagrams. In Chapter 6 they are the cornerstones for defining class operations, and in this chapter they are the cornerstones for defining role-based security. In the next chapter you will see how sequence diagrams are also the cornerstones for determining the test coverage of the system.

To be fully effective, the approach presented in this chapter imposes as a constraint that each external service must be represented by a boundary .NET implementation class, or must present a .NET interface. By external service you have to understand a third-party product that is being integrated into the application. The issues related to external systems and their boundary classes were discussed in detail in Chapter 6.

The approach presented can be applied with any .NET role-based security setup, relying on any type of authentication policy of the application: Windows, Forms, or Passport. In particular, within the case study of this book, it works in conjunction with the role-based security mechanism described in Chapter 6, which relies on Forms authentication.

Actors and Roles

In Chapter 3, one important activity in the development of the use case model was to create the actor model. The process presented in this book gives a lot of emphasis on the analysis of the actors and the development of a precise actor model. We have seen in Chapter 3 how a precise actor model impacts the detailed specification of the use cases, helping to define a cohesive and consistent set of use cases. A precise actor model is even more critical to the specification of role-based security, as each nonabstract actor in the model represents an actual role, as described in Chapter 3. Figure 8-1 depicts the actor model developed in Chapter 3.

Actors may be related with inheritance relationships, which define specialization of the responsibilities but also of the access rights of one actor relative to another. In the example of the case study, Admin inherits from Registered Buyer, which means that Admin can do everything that Registered Buyer can (e.g., shop), but can also do other things (e.g., manage accounts). Inheritance relationships between actors define a hierarchy of role definitions. If this hierarchy could be implemented in .NET, it would simplify the configuration of .NET role-based security. Indeed, if an operation is accessible by a Registered Buyer role, it is automatically accessible by an Admin role (e.g., because a Reg-

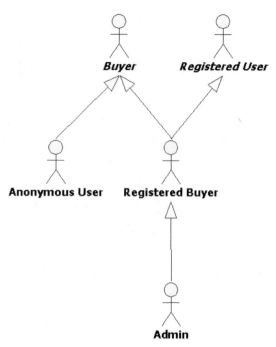

Figure 8-1: Actor model.

```
[PrincipalPermissionAttribute(SecurityAction.Demand, Role = "RegisteredBuyer")]
public void SubmitOrder(OrderOrderItemInfo dsCart, string stCreditCardNumber)
```

Figure 8-2: An ideal situation if .NET supported role inheritance.

```
[PrincipalPermissionAttribute(SecurityAction.Demand, Role = "RegisteredBuyer")]
[PrincipalPermissionAttribute(SecurityAction.Demand, Role = "Admin")]
public void SubmitOrder(OrderOrderItemInfo dsCart, string stCreditCardNumber)
```

Figure 8-3: Actor inheritance mapped to role configuration for .NET.

istered Buyer can submit an order, an Admin can also submit an order). Figure 8-2 presents the resulting .NET attribute adornment.

Unfortunately this is *not* the case in .NET, which means that you have to explicitly specify both roles in the access list of that specific operation, as depicted in Figure 8-3.

Analysis-Level Role-Based Security Model

The security model at the analysis level defines the accessibility of the analysis classes by the system actors, without consideration of specific operations on the classes. Thus, it does not directly relate to the .NET role-based security configuration. In this perspective, defining a security model at the analysis level might seem to be overkill, but the advantage of creating this model is that it effectively maps the system actors to the system functions they are using, in a matrix that defines a synthetic view of the analysis classes.

The objective of the security model at the analysis level is to decide which classes are accessible by each actor. This is done by carefully reviewing the sequence diagrams of the analysis model, which represent the interaction between an actor and the classes of the system, in the context of a use case. The assumption is that all use cases are modeled with interaction diagrams in the analysis model, as presented in Chapter 5. In these sequence diagrams, the actor is clearly identified as being the originator of the interaction. At this level

Table 8-1: Analysis role-based security matrix example.

Analysis Classes	Actor A	Actor B	Actor C
Class 1	X	X	
Class 2		X	X

of detail, it is sufficient to specify an actor's access to a specific class by virtue of the class being in a direct message path initiated by the actor.

That excludes classes that are represented on the sequence diagram but are interacting with another actor (e.g. in the Create Account use case the initiating actor is Anonymous User, but at the end of the interaction, the Account Home page is accessed by the Registered Buyer actor; see Figure 5-10 in Chapter 5). Thus, this class is not in the direct message path of Anonymous User and cannot appear to be accessible by that actor. In reality, most of the time there is only one actor per sequence diagram; a general rule is that every class participating in a specific sequence diagram should be accessible by the role associated with the actor.

The representation of the role-based security model is a matrix where the first column lists the analysis classes of the system, while the first row lists the actors. When an actor has access to one class, the intersection of the actor column and the class row should be marked with an X. Table 8-1 is a conceptual example of the analysis role-based security matrix.

Design-Level Role-Based Security Model

The approach for developing the security model at the design level is very similar to the one at the analysis level. At this level, you create the security matrix by examining the sequence diagrams developed in the design model. The only difference is that for this model you need to be very granular and consider not only the implementation classes, but also their operations. For this reason, the representation of the role-based security model is a matrix where the first column lists the implementation classes of the system, and for each class the second column lists its operations. The first row lists the actors. When a class operation is in the direct message path of an interaction initiated by an actor, the intersection of the actor column and the operation row should be marked with an X. Note that in the sequence diagram you might also be tempted for clarification reasons to represent some calls to private operations. This is not a good practice, but in any case it is important to note that for the security matrix you should list only public operations.

One exception is the code-behind classes of Web forms and controls. For these classes, the .NET role-based security adornments should be placed on the class itself (which is public by essence), rather than the class operations. Indeed, in these classes, the various user interface events are represented by protected operation, in order to be accessible by the Web form or control, which inherits from the corresponding class defined in the code-behind files. This is controlled by a .NET mechanism, as discussed in Chapter 6. This approach makes sense if you think that a Web page or control is displayed as an atomic unit to the user. Note that you may choose to be more granular if you decide to take advantage of role-based security in order to selectively display or hide user interface elements on the forms. But this discussion is in the realm of application security and is not incompatible with the following approach. Table 8-2 is a conceptual example of the design role-based security matrix.

The following two remarks are applicable if you use a UML design tool that implements an extensibility model:

- It is possible to develop a tool extension that is able to step through the implementation classes and the sequence diagrams and automatically generate both the analysis- and design-level security matrixes.

- It is also possible to develop a tool extension that takes as input the design-level security matrix and generates the .NET role-based security adornments to the code of the implementation class operations.

Table 8-2: Design role-based security matrix example.

Implementation Classes	Operation	Actor A	Actor B	Actor C
Class 1	Operation 1	X		
Class 1	Operation 2	X	X	
Class 1	Operation 3	X		X
Class 2	Operation 1	X		
Class 2	Operation 2		X	

Case Study

Applying the approach to the Create Account use case, this section will demonstrate the development of the role-based security matrix, first at the analysis level and then at the design level. The actor model used has been reviewed in the Approach and is depicted in Figure 8-1. The actors that are of interest in the subsequent discussion are Anonymous User and Registered Buyer.

Analysis-Level Role-Based Security Model

The main input artifacts for this activity are the sequence diagrams of the analysis model for the Create Account use case. For this use case we have already reviewed the sequence diagram describing the basic flow of events (in Figure 5-10 of Chapter 5). Note that at the same time this diagram presents all classes involved in validation, thus effectively also covering the "User Enters Invalid User Account Information" alternate flow. As a reminder, at this level of analysis we are only interested in participating classes and not class operations. A second diagram, depicted in Figure 8-4, describes the flow of events for the "User Cancels Request" alternate flow.

A careful review of these diagrams permits us to define the analysis role-based security matrix in Table 8-3.

Reviewing this matrix we can make the following remarks:

- The accessibility of Home by Anonymous User is established by reviewing the diagram in Figure 8-4, though the narrative of the basic flow diagram also implicitly defines it. Thus this accessibility could also appear in the basic flow diagram, if we had chosen to represent the screens that Anonymous User can access in order to initiate the interaction for the basic flow of the use case.

- The Account Home is not accessible by Anonymous User because it is not in any direct message path of an interaction initiated by this actor. Instead it is in a direct message path of an interaction sourcing from Registered Buyer. One could argue that in the mechanics of the implementation, Account Home is actually in a message path of Anonymous User as it is the same series of operation calls that will lead to that screen. But this way of reasoning does not take into account the fact that during this series of

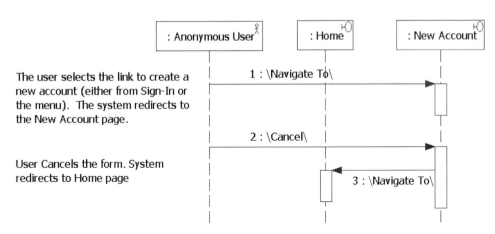

The user selects the link to create a new account (either from Sign-In or the menu). The system redirects to the New Account page.

User Cancels the form. System redirects to Home page

Figure 8-4: Analysis model sequence diagram for the Create Account use case: User Cancels Request.

calls there is a transformation of the role of the current user from Anonymous User to Registered Buyer. In contrast, this role transformation is represented effectively in the design of the sequence diagram.

■ Because Admin is a kind of Registered Buyer, and in the perspective that the .NET role-based security mechanism does not support inheritance,

Table 8-3: Analysis role-based security matrix review.

Analysis Classes	Anonymous User	Registered Buyer	Admin
New Account	X		
New Account Verify	X		
Account Home		X	X
Home	X		
Create Account Dispatcher	X		
Credit Card System	X		
Account Manager	X		
User Account	X		
Credit Card	X		
User Group	X		

when marking a class as accessible by the Registered User role, it is important to mark that class as also accessible by the Admin role.

Design-Level Role-Based Security Model

For this level of the security model, the main input artifacts are the sequence diagrams of the design model for the Create Account use case. For this use case we have defined four sequence diagrams, presented in Figures 6-23, 6-25, 6-26, and 6-27 in Chapter 6. A fifth diagram, depicted in Figure 8-5, describes the flow of events for the "User Cancels Request" alternate flow. This diagram is very similar to Figure 8-4, with the difference that it references actual implementation classes and operations.

A careful review of these diagrams permits us to define the design role-based security matrix in Table 8-4. The same remark applies to the Admin role in the analysis-level security matrix, hence the accessibility of Home_Account by the Admin role.

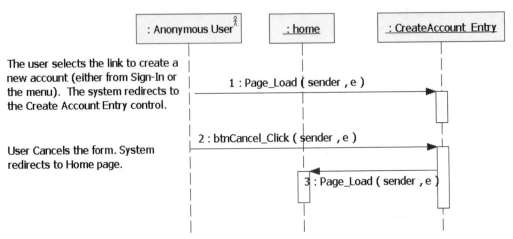

Figure 8-5: Design model sequence diagram for the Create Account use case: User Cancels Request.

Table 8-4: Role-based security matrix example.

Class	Operation	Anonymous User	Registered Buyer	Admin
CreateAccount_Entry	Class Definition	X		
CreateAccount_Verify	Class Definition	X		
Home_Account	Class Definition		X	X
Home	Class Definition	X		
CreateAccount Dispatcher	ProcessEvents	X		
AccountManager	ActivateUserAccount			
	CreateAccount	X		
	DeactivateUserAccount			
	GetCreditCardInfo			
	GetCreditCardInfoBy CardNumber			
	GetUserAccountByUniqueId			
	GetUserAccountByUserId	X		
	GetUserGroupByUniqueId			
	SetUserUIDToGroupId	X		
	UpdateAccount			
	ValidateAccount			
CreditCardManager	ChargeTransactionFee			
	IsCreditCardValid	X		
UserAccount	Create	X		
	FindByUserId	X		
	FindByUniqueId			
	Update	X		
CreditCard	Create	X		
	FindByCardNumber			
	FindByUniqueId			
	Update	X		
UserGroup	Create	X		
	FindByUniqueId			
	Update	X		

Summary

In this chapter we reviewed the activities related to the development of the role-based security model. Role-based security is a powerful feature of the .NET platform that can help address the application server security of your software system, with no impact on the code structure, as it is based on .NET attributes. The approach presented in this chapter presents a systematic approach for deciding how to configure role-based security for a .NET application. The systematization facilitates the work of software architects that have to make these decisions and effectively introduces a rational dimension to this activity.

Within this activity you produce two artifacts: analysis role-based security matrix and design role-based security matrix. The principal input artifacts for this activity are the actor model from the use case analysis, the analysis model sequence diagrams, and the design model sequence diagrams. The approach promotes the creation of two levels of security modeling, both represented by a security matrix. The security model at the analysis level is a coarse specification and represents the accessibility of the various actors to each analysis classes as a whole. At the design level, the security model considers the accessibility of the actors for every implementation class and operation.

The cornerstones for developing both the analysis- and design-level security matrix are the sequence diagrams, and the assumption is that all use cases have been completely specified with sequence diagrams. An actor has accessibility to every class/operation that is in a direct message path of an interaction it has initiated.

If your UML design tool defines an extensibility model, it is possible to develop a tool extension that automatically creates these security matrixes, as well as generate the appropriate .NET attributes adornments to the implementation classes and operations.

Chapter 9

Testing

Introduction

Along with security, testing is another major topic in software development. Without rigorous testing, there is no possible assertion of the quality of a system, and all organizations involved in software development are aware of the importance of testing. Unfortunately, today, when it comes to address the issues that define the testing discipline, either in a process or in a project, more often than not you will be observing a very craftsman-like situation.

This is paradoxical when you think that 20 or 30 years ago testing was a very rigorous discipline. The explanation is very simple: 30 years ago most software-intensive systems were strategic solutions, enjoying lots of resources and with very stringent requirements on quality. Today, a lot of systems fulfill tactical business objectives, in a very competitive environment, with very tight timeframes and limited budgets. No wonder that over that period, three-quarters of software automation projects have failed, being either over budget, over time, of poor quality, or scrapped altogether (you can find more precise figures in the Standish Group CHAOS report; see `http://www.standishgroup.com/chaos/index.html`). Note, however, that even the well-tested strategic projects from long ago tended to go over budget and over time.

Nonetheless, the most conscious organizations are generally achieving a good level of quality in the related activities, but often at the price of excessive allocation of resources (people and time). The good news is that the situation is generally improving, as the software development industry matures in the six dimensions described in Chapter 6: technology, tools, methods/techniques, processes, people, and organization. This improvement is apparent in the comparison between the 1994 and 1998 figures published by the Standish Group.

The objective of this chapter is to demonstrate how a seemingly peripheral issue like testing can actually be integrated within an overall engineering approach to software development, and how to implement traceability for testing artifacts as for any other type of artifacts. The software engineering approach presented in this book can help you achieve a high level of organizational performance in the testing activities, as defined by two elements:

- Quality of testing, by defining techniques and methods ensuring the complete test coverage of all the requirements of the system, verifiable by the capability to trace the results to the requirements.
- Efficiency, by defining a rigorous process for testing, but also by enabling the automation of a large number of tasks.

This chapter will focus on functional testing, as a means of completing the exploration of the functional aspects of the development of a software system. Other test topics (which we will not discuss) would be:

- Performance testing. For example, the number of concurrent sessions that a single Web server can support at a 1- and 5-second response time for known page composition.
- Stress testing. For example, the number of concurrent sessions that a single Web server can maintain, while "gracefully" degrading its performance. "Gracefully" in this context means without loss of data or emergence of error conditions in the system itself.
- Scalability testing and capacity planning. This involves increasing the load at the same time as augmenting the infrastructure and verifying that the system response is kept within the set targets.
- Availability and resilience:

- ❏ Failover, or how long it takes to happen, whether any transactions are lost/fail in the meantime.

- ❏ That a single failure does not cause loss of all of a certain type of system components.

- ❏ Whether the level of service degradation can be controlled (e.g., max sessions, threads per process, etc.).

- ■ Security testing. For example, technical vulnerability exploitation (brute force attacks, buffer overflows, replay attacks, session hijacking) and denial of service attacks.

- ■ Acceptance testing. Representatives of the user stakeholders test the complete system in order to assess readiness for operation.

Two other topics that will not be discussed are configuration management and defect tracking, which address issues like staging of the test configuration, test versioning, and bug tracking. Though very important and interesting, a discussion on these topics will drive the focus away from the core concern of this book, which is the process of refinement of the functional specifications. Due to the vastness of the subject, it is impossible to cover all of the testing discipline within one single chapter. For further enlightened reading on the topic I recommend *A Practical Guide to Testing Object-Oriented Software*; for in-depth coverage of advanced methods and techniques, see *Testing Object-Oriented Systems*. You will also find important insight on testing as part of the overall software development process in *The Rational Unified Process: An Introduction*.

Functional testing takes a black box or behavioral perspective to testing. This perspective consists of completely disregarding any possible knowledge of the way the unit/system operates internally. This is in contrast to the white box or structural perspective, where the test definition takes into account the understanding of the inner works of the unit/system. Among the tools that are used for white box testing are the code debuggers. The white box approach is often more appropriate in situations where the requirements are not well defined for the unit. This is certainly not the case when you apply the practical process described in this book, but the reality is that to achieve a practical and effective approach to testing, it is a good practice to combine the two approaches.

In this chapter we will consider two stages of functional testing:

- ■ Unit test. A unit is the smallest amount of code that is allocated to one developer. A good practice in an OOAD context is to define a unit to be the code for one implementation class. The rationale for this choice is that a class defines the smallest self-contained unit, encapsulating its code and data. As such, it is also a good practice to define it as the smallest unit of responsibility for a developer. In unit testing, any call to another implementation class outside the unit is replaced with stubs or simulators. Calls to .NET framework classes or trusted components (external systems with .NET managed interfaces) are maintained as is. Calls by other implementation classes are replaced with drivers. Thus, the unit is tested in isolation. Unit testing is a responsibility of the developers, as it is most likely to take a white box testing approach, making extensive use of debugger tools.

- System test, which considers the whole solution as a unit. Within one specific development iteration, the system test will cover the relevant use cases, as well as all use cases from previous iterations. This entails applying regression tests for the test cases that cover the use cases of the previous iterations. System testing is the responsibility of the testers, defined as a separate team.

As you will see later in this chapter, both unit test and system test artifacts trace back to use cases through the use case scenarios: unit tests through the design of the implementation classes in sequence diagrams, and system tests through the test cases. Both sequence diagrams and test cases are based on use case scenarios. Thus, the two groups of workers involved in these activities have a common reference source of knowledge that defines their objectives, and they can easily achieve a common understanding in their communication.

As a final remark for this Introduction, it is not in the scope of this chapter, or of the book in general, to review any specific test automation tools, either for unit test or system test. The objective is to present you with the concepts involved in the testing activities, as well as practical methods and techniques to apply.

Approach

The approach presented puts the test development effort in a parallel track with the design and code efforts. The input artifacts for test activities, as for all the design activities, are use case descriptions, as we take the perspective of the functional aspects of software development. After all, this is a use case-driven process, and use cases are the original representation of the system knowledge, defining the system requirements and specifications, the code, the documentation, and the tests. In reality you will see in this chapter that test cases and use cases are tightly related. Indeed, the overall idea of the approach is to map the use cases onto test cases.

Test Cases

As test cases proceed from use cases, the activity of specifying them can start very early in the overall development process, as soon as the use cases of the current iteration are specified in detail. The best timing is to start developing the test cases along the use case detail descriptions. However, because use cases are likely to be updated throughout the development of the analysis model, you must be aware that you will need to maintain the consistency of test cases with the use cases. On the other hand, having the test cases completed and stable, along with the use cases at the end of the analysis model and before developing the design model, will be useful in order to start testing the implementation classes that are developed in parallel with the design model.

Test cases are the basic components of testing. A test case is defined as a set of data inputs, execution conditions, and expected results. You can think of each test case as representing a use case scenario, or a complete path through one use case. Each use case scenario involves some or all steps of the basic flow of events and possibly one or more alternate flow of events. The above definition of test cases is very close to the definition of sequence diagrams in Chapter 6, and a practical approach to develop test cases is to create at least one test case for each use case scenario represented by a sequence diagram. Note that this does not mean using the sequence diagrams to describe the test cases, as this approach would effectively define a white box test. It does mean to base the test case on the same description of the use case scenario that defines the sequence diagram.

As a practical approach, each use case scenario is focused on a particular flow of events (basic or alternates). Consequently, defining test cases from a use case scenario effectively means to create one or more test cases for each documented flow of events of the use case. For this reason, all test cases that correspond to one use case scenario define a class of test cases that specify the same execution conditions, differing only in their input data and the results. At the same time, the activity of creating test cases is also an opportunity to unveil important use case scenarios, beyond those defined by the simple enumeration of the use case flow of events. In this perspective, test cases are also a very useful validation and consistency check for the use case scenarios.

In summary, a use case will map to one or more test cases that exercise its basic and alternate flow of events. Also, a use case maps to one or more implementation classes and their collaborations that realize its basic and alternate flows of events. Thus, the objective of mapping use cases to test cases is to ensure that each test case exercises the implementation classes that realize one or more flows of events of the related use case. Achieving this objective will ensure that the testing covers the system specification as defined by the use cases. Figure 9-1 depicts the concepts discussed in this section and their relationships. Note that in the selected approach, any use case scenario exercises only one or two flows of events: one when only the basic flow is involved, two when the basic flow and one of the alternate flows are involved. In this diagram you will also notice the concept of Test Scenario, which is a compound of test cases that represent a complex user task or a complete user session. Test scenarios are discussed in their own section later in this chapter.

All test cases of a specific use case scenario share the same definition of execution conditions, which represent the set of data elements that is involved in the corresponding use case scenario. These conditions can be represented in a test case matrix that is specific to the related use case scenario (see the magazine article "Generating Test Cases From Use Cases"). Table 9-1 is the matrix

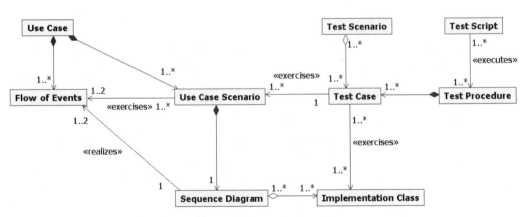

Figure 9-1: Concepts involved in testing and their relationships.

Table 9-1: Test Case Matrix: Definitions of the Execution Condition and Test Results

Use Case	Create Account		
Use Case Scenario	CreateAccount_Entry validation		
Test Case ID	TC4	TC5	TC6
Condition	Username exists	Passwords do not match	Invalid card expiration date
Username	I	N/A	V
Password	V	V	V
Verify Password	V	I	V
E-mail address	V	N/A	V
Name on Credit Card	V	N/A	V
Card Number	V	N/A	V
Card Type	V	N/A	V
Expiration	V	N/A	I
Street Address	V	N/A	V
City	V	N/A	V
State	V	N/A	V
ZIP/Postal Code	V	N/A	V
Country	V	N/A	V
Expected Results	Message displayed:	Message displayed:	Message displayed:
	This user already exists. Please enter another user.	*The 2 password fields do not match.*	*Expiration date must be between MM1/yyy1 and MM2/yyy2.*

for the "CreateAccount_Entry validation" use case scenario of the Create Account use case. Note that the use case scenario should correspond to a collaboration instance (containing its sequence diagrams) in the design model.

In this matrix we do not enter data values but only an indication of which fields are valid (V), invalid (I), or indifferent (N/A). In TC5 it is sufficient to enter a valid first password and a different verify password to get the expected result, thus all other fields are indifferent. Although there will be other error messages, they are not of any interest for the test case. The above matrix is partial, as it does not cover all the possible error conditions that may occur. More test cases are needed, so that each condition has at least an invalid indication in one test case column.

The next step is to define actual test data in place of the indications on the test conditions. The same matrix template is used for this purpose (see Table 9-2).

In the test case matrix, the expected results describe the state of the system from a user perspective, thus keeping the black box view of the system. They describe in all details the state of the application and any other element of the system environment that is affected as a result of the test activities (e.g., message ABC on the screen, water pump XYZ is now on, message to abc@xyz.com sent and will be received within X hours).

Table 9-2: Test Case Matrix: Input Data

Use Case	Create Account		
Use Case Scenario	CreateAccount_Entry validation		
Test Case ID	TC4	TC5	TC6
Condition	Username exists	Passwords do not match	Invalid card expiration date
Username	testbuyer01	N/A	testbuyer10
Password	testbuyer01pwd	testbuyer10pwd	testbuyer10pwd
Verify Password	testbuyer01pwd	Test	testbuyer10pwd
E-mail address	testbuyer01@ softgnsosis.com	N/A	testbuyer10@ softgnsosis.com
Name on Credit Card	testbuyer01	N/A	testbuyer10
Card Number	1111222233330001	N/A	1111222233330010
Card Type	MC	N/A	MC
Expiration	02/04	N/A	02/15
Street Address	1, High Street	N/A	1, High Street
City	London	N/A	London
State		N/A	
ZIP/Postal Code	W1	N/A	W1
Country	UK	N/A	UK
Expected Results	Message displayed: *This user already exists. Please enter another user.*	Message displayed: *The 2 password fields do not match.*	Message displayed: *Expiration date must be between 09/2002 and 09/2007*

Test Procedures

The test case specifications are not enough by themselves to conduct a test run. Test procedures define the steps and environmental conditions (system and application) that need to be in place in order to execute one or more test cases. Test procedures also define the steps to analyze the results. A test procedure can describe the execution of one or more test cases, as depicted in Figure 9-1. The reality is that most of the time you should expect to define a one-to-one map of a test case to a test procedure. In this perspective it is often more effective to create two test procedures that are very similar than to try to merge the two procedures in one.

The various parts of the execution of test procedures are automated by developing test scripts either by coding them or using automated tools to generate them. Automated test tools generate the test scripts by capturing the user actions with the system. Ideally, test procedures should be completely automated.

It is useful to define a test procedure template, as it brings structure to your thinking when describing the steps for testing (see Table 9-3).

The test procedure steps derive directly from the flow of events defining the use case scenario that the test case represents. A simple way to think of a test case is as an instantiation of a use case flow of events, thus effectively using the same description for the execution steps, but imposing on you the requirement to think and document every detail of the state of the system before and after the execution of the test.

The test case matrix effectively defines the combination of data that will be used for a specific test procedure. Note that because a set of test cases within a particular test case matrix correspond to one use case scenario, it is possible that they will also share the same test procedure, and consequently the same test scripts. But in general every test case will potentially have its own test procedure.

In parallel with the test case definitions you must also maintain a repository of the tests executed, in which iteration, and what the result of the test was. If the result did not match the expected state of the system and/or data, an incident will be raised with the developers to investigate the problem. Note that incidents fall into two broad categories:

- True defects, where some code or system configuration has to be modified.
- False alarms, arising from erroneous test case definitions.

In the case of a false alarm, after investigation, the defect along with its assessment shall be transmitted to the test team that will need to amend the test case definition and run the test case again before closing the defect report.

Table 9-3: Test procedure template.

Test procedure	Name of the test procedure *(for identification)*
Related test case(s)	The identification of the test case(s) that this procedure covers *(useful for traceability and assessment of the coverage of functional testing to the system specifications)*
Initial state of the system before the test case starts	Describe in all details the state of the application as well as any element of the system environment that is of importance during the test; e.g., connection to a bar-code reader, particular HTTP port enabled *(useful to avoid false test failure incidents due to inadequacy of the test assumptions with the current system environment and state).*
State of the data used by the system before the test case starts	Describe in all details the state of the data in the system, as it has to be present before the test is conducted. This may entail describing the steps to prepare the data and reference of any automated script or another document that describes the procedure to prepare the data for the particular test *(useful to ensure that the test does not generate false test failure incidents due to inadequacy of test assumptions with available system data).*
Test procedure steps	Describe in all details the steps that the user has to follow. Be very specific, referencing the specific buttons or links to click, or input fields to fill. The data itself is one of the data sets from the test case descriptions covered by the procedure.
Expected final state of the system after the test case finishes	Complementary description of the test case results. This after the test case finishes description is optional and focuses on the elements of the system environment that are not specified within the corresponding use case *(useful in order to add a white box perspective to the test).*
Expected state of the data used by the system after the test case finishes	Describe in every detail the state of the data in the system as a result of the test. This may entail referencing extended documentation on how to extract the data from the system; e.g., a specific SQL query to execute *(useful in order to add a white box perspective to the test. Note that the related scripts need to be created by the developers.).*

Effectively this procedure consists of handing over the responsibility of correcting the defect, while the overall defect management and resolution procedure stays the same as in the case of a true defect.

Test Coverage Matrix

From the above discussion it is straightforward to trace every flow of event of every use case to a test case. But considering the discussion on test case mapping to implementation classes, a practical question that springs to mind is how to ensure that every operation of every implementation class is participating in a test case.

The indirect and necessary answer to this question is to consider the sequence diagram of a use case scenario, representing a particular flow of events of a use case, and list the implementation classes with their operations involved in the collaboration defined in the design model. As this particular flow of events has a corresponding test case, the implication is that the test case does exercise the corresponding implementation classes and the operations involved in the sequence diagram. A first evaluation of test coverage can be documented by using a simple matrix, named the test coverage matrix, where you represent all implementation classes with all their operations in the first two columns, along with all the test cases on the first row. Then you mark with an X every cell where an implementation class is involved in the test case(s) corresponding to the design model sequence diagram(s) where the implementation class is used.

At the same time, as the matrix effectively references all units of the system, it is the best place to track the completeness of unit test definitions. The other advantage is that you can quickly identify test case data to use for the unit test, as it will be some derivation of the test case data that covers the corresponding class operation. Table 9-4 is a conceptual example of a test coverage matrix.

In the example in Table 9-4 you can identify a problem with the operation OB2 of implementation class CB, as it seems that it is not exercised in any test case. As described in the design model in Chapter 6, the process of discovering class operations is based on developing the sequence diagrams for each possible flow of events of a use case, represented in a use case scenario. Consequently, an operation that is not covered by a test case can only mean that there is a test case missing for each flow of events where the operation is used.

Table 9-4: Test coverage matrix example.

Class	Operation	Unit Test	Test Case A	Test Case B	Test Case C
CA	OA1	X	X		X
	OA2	X		X	X
CB	OB1	X		X	
	OB2	X			
	OB3	X		X	
CC	OC1		X		

A second problem involves the OC1 operation of implementation class CC, where you can identify that a unit test has yet to be defined. Thus, the test coverage matrix is a powerful validation technique for test coverage. There should be only one test coverage matrix for all the system, in order to use it as a synthetic view, or dashboard of the state of completeness of the testing effort.

Continuing the investigation of the above question on assessing the test coverage of every operation, a direct answer that would complement the above test coverage matrix would be to use a code coverage tool. This type of tool can identify the lines of code in the program that are never executed during testing. The approach is very simple and consists of running the code coverage tool while you execute a particular test case. Then you analyze the results produced by the tool and verify in the test coverage matrix that all of the classes and operations that have an X for the corresponding test case have been executed during the run. If not, you must investigate whether this situation is due to the definition of the test case or the definition of the sequence diagram.

Applying both of the above techniques will give you the necessary and sufficient conditions to positively assert the question of the test coverage of implementation classes. Note that using a test coverage tool is part of a white box approach to testing, as these tools are effectively analyzing the structure of the classes and operations. Nonetheless, the approach described demonstrates the complementarities between the two techniques. Although white box testing is more in the realm of the developers, who have an intimate understanding of the inner workings and structure of the code, you can find code coverage tools like Rational PureCoverage that integrate transparently with automated testing tools in a black box approach to testing, thus effectively bridging the gap between back box and white box testing and integrating the testing activities of testers and developers.

Test Scenarios

Test cases are used as building blocks for test scenarios, which represent plausible usage of the system by end users in terms of a series of tasks that the user will want to execute. They are useful in describing typical user sessions, involving a sequence of use cases, some of which might be repeated; for

Table 9-5: Test scenario template.

Test Scenario	Name of the test scenario *(for identification)*
Purpose	Describe the rationale why this scenario was defined.
Description	Describe what this scenario does.
Test type	Functional/Load/Stress/Performance/Security…
Test cases used	The list of test cases involved in the scenario. Reference the test case names.
Initial state of the system before the test scenario starts	Describe in all details the state of the application as well as any element of the system environment that is of importance during the test; e.g., connection to a bar-code reader, particular HTTP port enabled.
State of the data used by the system before the scenario starts	Describe in all details the state of the data in the system, as it has to be present before the test is conducted. This may entail describing the steps to prepare the data and reference any automated script or another document that describes the procedure to prepare the data for the particular test.
Test scenario steps	Enumerate the test cases that have to be applied. Identify repeating sets of test cases and how many repetitions; for example: 1. Execute test case: A Execute 2 followed by 3 for 7 times. 2. Execute test case: B 3. Execute test case: C 4. Execute test case: D
Additional directives and information to collect	Any extra details on the test execution and what information to collect or verify in order to assess the success of the test.

example, when the user shops for books, a test scenario can be composed of sign-in, repeat N times (browse catalogue; select books), check-out, sign-out.

Test scenarios are particularly useful when developing load tests where you should create a representative mix of use cases that are likely to happen in parallel during normal system operation. As test cases are the building blocks of test scenarios, these will be composed of one or more test cases. In test scenarios you might also mix the basic flow of events of some use cases, with the alternate flows of other use cases in order to verify that integrity of the data is maintained. Similar to the test cases, it is desirable to define a practical template for test scenarios.

I will not cover test scenarios in any more detail in this book, as they do not bring significantly more insight than test cases to the discussion of functional testing.

Unit Test

A unit test is most likely to entail using a combination of white box and black box approaches. As seen in the Introduction, the black box approach to unit testing mandates that all implementation classes stub all the calls to other implementation classes that are external to the unit under consideration. As a small reminder and a matter of practicality, the strongly typed DataSet classes described in Chapter 6 are considered as .NET infrastructure classes and consequently trusted to be working correctly during unit tests. Stubbing the implementation classes is quite easy to achieve for three reasons:

- The class operation called has already been defined, as per applying the approach of Chapter 6. Thus, the stub structure already exists.
- By virtue of the design pattern described in Chapter 6, the only implementation classes that should ever be returned to the caller are the strongly typed DataSets, as representing system data. As these classes are trusted, you can create instances inside the stub and populate them with the appropriate data needed for the unit test.
- Other classes that need to be returned are .NET framework classes, which are also trusted and can easily be created and populated inside the stub with the appropriate data for the unit test.

The first step for black box unit testing consists of systematically creating stubs for all implementation classes as soon as these classes and their operations are defined in the design model. Figure 9-2 gives an example of a stubbed class structure. Note in the implementation namespace the reference to a ".Stubs" namespace to be used for the definition of the actual class implementation.

Just copy within the same implementation file the structure of the implementation class, but under a different namespace that has a ".Stubs" suffix to the actual implementation class namespace. The calling units will need to reference that namespace in place of the default namespace of the class. This simplifies the work for system integration, as you only need to take out all the ".Stubs" suffixes of the "using" clauses in each code file in order to start calling the actual implementation classes. The other advantage is that it prevents the stub class definitions from getting in the way and hogging the implementation models, as they are kept separate under different namespace packages, as seen in Chapter 7.

All operations definitions within the stub class definition remain the same as for the real class. The code of a stubbed operation has as a primary objective to create and populate return objects with static data. In order to do so, it is very useful to get inspiration from the test case data that is defined for the test cases that cover the same operation, as per the test coverage matrix. At the same time, the structure of the stubbed code also defines the initial structure of the corresponding actual class, with the constraint of not calling to any other actual or stubbed implementation class. Adopting this approach is helpful in two ways:

- It helps you think of the structure of the actual implementation class and its operations. In this perspective it is a complementary design step.
- It helps to create a stub that simulates various normal or abnormal conditions, but sourcing exclusively from the class structure. You should ban any attempt to consider what error conditions are carried over from downstream calls. Defining normal and abnormal conditions is helpful for improving the testing of the calling class.

When all stubs are created, they are made available to all developers to use while they implement the units they have been assigned. The next step is to create unit tests for each unit. It is interesting to make a parallel with what happens in Extreme Programming (XP), where the process also takes a similar approach in putting even more of an emphasis on specifying test cases as the basis for coding.

Unit tests are effectively realized by code components that represent the concept of test drivers discussed in the Introduction. The general pattern of a test driver is to initialize the required objects, execute a call to the operation

```
namespace BooksREasy.UserAcctMgr.UserAcctMgrBLL
{
    using System;
    using BooksREasy.Common.UtilityClasses;
    using BooksREasy.UserAcctMgr.UserAcctMgrDAL.Stubs;

    public class AccountManager : MarshalbyRefObject
        /// <summary>
        /// getUserAccountByUserId: Locates the user account with the specified userId.
        /// </summary>
        /// <param name="UserId">userID of the user to retrieve user account information for.</param>
        /// <returns>Typed UserInfo dataset that contains the UserAccount record with a matching userID.</returns>
        public UserInfo getUserAccountByUserId (string userId)
        {
            //
            //TODO: implement the operation
            //
        }
    }
}
//Stubs
namespace BooksREasy.UserAcctMgr.UserAcctMgrBLL.Stubs
{
    using BooksREasy.Common.UtilityClasses;
    public class AccountManager
    {
        public UserInfo getUserAccountByUserId (string userId)
        {
            UserInfo dsUser = new UserInfo();
            if (userId=="testbuyer10")
            {
                dsUser.UserAccount.AddUserAccountRow(dsUser.UserAccount.NewUserAccountRow());
                dsUser.UserAccount[0].UserId=testbuyer10;
                dsUser.UserAccount[0].Password="testbuyer10pwd";
                dsUser.UserAccount[0].Email="testbuyer10@softgnosis.com";
                dsUser.UserAccount[0].Addr1="1, High Street";
                dsUser.UserAccount[0].City="London";
                dsUser.UserAccount[0].Country="UK"
                dsUser.UserAccount[0].SecretNumber="1111";
                dsUser.UserAccount[0].State="";
                dsUser.UserAccount[0].Status=CommonKeyWords.ACTIVE;
                dsUser.UserAccount[0].Zip="W1";
            }
            return dsUser;
        }
    }
}
```

Figure 9-2: Defining a ".Stubs" namespace for each implementation class.

under test, and check the state of the returned objects. It is also a good practice to keep the unit test code along with the definition of its corresponding class and stub, using a namespace suffixed with ".Tests" in a similar way as for stubs. Figure 9-3 presents test drivers.

Note that you also need to have a utility application to run these tests and manage results. At this stage it is useful to use a unit test tool to automate this activity, which brings two advantages:

- It defines a structure for documenting the unit test, including the test code.
- It defines an environment to execute the tests and track test results.

At the time of this writing, I have evaluated two unit test tools that were specifically designed for the .NET platform: Nunit and HarnessIt. Both take advantage of the attribute-based programming of .NET.

Having defined the stubbed implementation classes and the test drivers, we are in the position to test the unit in complete isolation, as required by a black box approach to testing.

In reality, it is not always easy or effective to implement a unit test exclusively using a black box approach. This is due mainly to the inherent complexity of the underlying .NET technological framework. As much as it

```
namespace BooksREasy.UserAcctMgr.UserAcctMgrBLL.Tests
{
    using System;
    using System.Diagnostics;
    using BooksREasy.Common.UtilityClasses;

    public class AccountManager_getUserAccountByUserId_Test
    {
        public void success()
        {
            UserInfo dsUser =new AccountManager() .getUserAccountByUserId("testbuyer10");
            Debug.Assert (dsUser.UserAccount.Rows.Count == 1
                && dsUser.UserAccount[0].Status.Equals (CommonKeyWords.ACTIVE), "Success");
        }

        public void fail_Invalid_UserId()
        {
            UserInfo dsUser =new AccountManager().getUserAccountByUserId("dummyUserId");
            Debug.Assert (dsUser.UserAccount.Rows.Count == 0,"Success");
        }
    }
}
```

Figure 9-3: Defining a ".Tests" namespace for each implementation class.

simplifies development, it also forces the designers to rely on the complex .NET mechanisms that work behind the scenes.

As an example, let's consider what happens when a UserControl is passed as an argument to a dispatcher class operation. If you want to apply a pure black box approach to the unit test, you need to completely isolate the class operation by creating a driver to call it. But then it is your responsibility to somehow create and initialize a UserControl class in order to use it as a parameter to the called operation. This is not a very practical and efficient usage of your time. The reality is that specifically for unit tests you have to be practical and not hesitate to take a white box approach to testing when it is appropriate. White box testing involves using debugger tools.

Thus, a definition of an overall approach for unit testing would be to start with a black box approach and complement it with a white box approach for the complex situations. At the same time you should be very conscious to document the unit tests, either by virtue of using a unit test tool or with documents or code annotations describing the tests. This is particularly important for white box testing, which is largely a manual process involving debugging procedures.

You also need to identify and acknowledge some dependencies in the timing of the development of the implementation classes, in order to take advantage of existing parts of the system, as the previous example suggests. Because of the very nature of unit tests, these dependencies often go in the inverse direction of the implementation dependencies defined by the sequence diagrams of the class collaborations (e.g., in the design model, a UserControl class depends on a dispatcher class).

Fortunately, this is not limiting, as during the design of sequence diagrams you will define the operations of the dependent classes based on the needs of the calling classes (e.g., the dispatcher class operation called by the UserControl class will already have been defined by the time you need to code its implementation). Thus, before developing the code of a class operation, you can already define a unit test for that operation, as well as have a test driver to test it. The only apparent limitation is that you do not completely control the test driver, as the call generated is partly the responsibility of the .NET framework. This situation is not limiting either, because of the assumption made in the Introduction of this chapter to trust the .NET components. The only impact is that for documenting the test you have to capture the data created by the .NET framework, instead of defining it beforehand.

System Test

In a simple and sufficient view for the discussion of this chapter, the system test consists of executing all the test cases defined so far for all the iterations of the system. Indeed, as described earlier, test cases are finalized at the same time as use cases. Thus, when the development team has developed the code implementing the use cases of the current iteration, it is possible for the test team to run the corresponding test cases. But at the same time, they also need to rerun all the test cases corresponding to use cases for the previous iterations, in order to ensure that the new state of system development has not introduced any defects to a previously defect-free system. This part of the testing is named regression testing.

It is clear by now that test cases will possibly be run a great number of times. For this reason, it is important to define a strategy to automate the test execution as much as possible. This entails using test automation tools, but also creating scripts that will set up the environment and initialize the system with the correct data. At the same time, you need to think of automation solutions to capture the state of the system and data upon completion of each test case.

Case Study

Applying the above approach to the case study, we will produce the functional test artifacts relating to the Create Account use case, focusing specifically on the basic flow of events.

Test Cases

The following test case matrix defines the three test cases that are sufficient to cover the use case scenario of creating a new user account. The start of the use case scenario specifies that the user accesses the Create Account screen either from a link on the main menu or through a button on the sign-in screen. Thus, the first two test cases, TC1 and TC2, are there to ensure that this part of the use case scenario is tested.

In TC3, the State field is indifferent because the system does not do any complex validation between the Country, the State, and the ZIP/Postal Code fields. This is the result of a simple system specification and not an error in the design (see Table 9-6). If more complex validation becomes a requirement, the

Table 9-6: Test Case Matrix: Definitions of the Execution Condition and Test Results

Use Case	Create Account		
Use Case Scenario	Basic Flow		
Test Case ID	TC1	TC2	TC3
Condition	Create Account is accessible from Sign-In	Create Account is accessible from menu item	Basic flow
Username	N/A	N/A	V
Password	N/A	N/A	V
Verify Password	N/A	N/A	V
E-mail address	N/A	N/A	V
Name on Credit Card	N/A	N/A	V
Card Number	N/A	N/A	V
Card Type	N/A	N/A	V
Expiration	N/A	N/A	V
Street Address	N/A	N/A	V
City	N/A	N/A	V
State	N/A	N/A	N/A
ZIP/Postal Code	N/A	N/A	V
Country	N/A	N/A	V
Expected Results	Create Account page is displayed.	Create Account page is displayed.	Account created and user signed in. Message displayed: *<userX> signed in.*

change will ripple throughout the use case specifications and system design to also impact the test case, which would then need to be changed to account for that new requirement (see Chapter 10 for the impact analysis of a change request involving the validation of the ZIP/Postal Code).

Table 9-7 is the test case matrix with the input data. Notice that we have not defined any data for the State field, as this is not a relevant concept for the United Kingdom.

Table 9-7: Test Case Matrix: Input data.

Use Case	Create Account		
Use Case Scenario	Basic Flow		
Test Case ID	TC1	TC2	TC3
Condition	Create Account is accessible from Sign-In	Create Account is accessible from menu item	Basic flow
Username	N/A	N/A	testbuyer10
Password	N/A	N/A	testbuyer10pwd
Verify Password	N/A	N/A	testbuyer10pwd
E-mail address	N/A	N/A	testbuyer10@ softgnsosis.com
Name on Credit Card	N/A	N/A	testbuyer10
Card Number	N/A	N/A	1111222233330010
Card Type	N/A	N/A	MC
Expiration	N/A	N/A	02/04
Street Address	N/A	N/A	1, High Street
City	N/A	N/A	London
State	N/A	N/A	
ZIP/Postal Code	N/A	N/A	W1
Country	N/A	N/A	UK
Expected Results	Create Account page is displayed.	Create Account page is displayed.	Account created and user signed in. Message displayed: *testbuyer10 signed in.*

Test Procedures

All the three test cases defined in the previous section can be executed within the test procedure defined in Table 9-8. It is a good practice to refer to the test cases within the test procedure steps in order to verify the consistency of the test procedure definition. The right mindset to acquire in order to develop test procedures is to consider every detail to be important.

In the test procedure in Table 9-8, Step 2 references TC3 as the sole test case data that is available for that step. In another situation where more than one test case data could be used for the same test procedure (e.g., TCxyz), a simple way to indicate alternate usage would be to write the step as: *At the*

Table 9-8: Create Account—Basic Flow test procedure.

Test Procedure	Create Account—Basic Flow
Related test case(s)	TC1, TC2, TC3
	■ Initial state of the system before the test case starts The test site is up and running
	■ A Web browser is open on the test machine, pointing to the test site. No user is signed in for this browser session.
State of the data used by the system	■ The user testbuyer10 does not exist in the BooksREasy before the test case starts system.

Test procedure steps	1. The Create Account use case is accessible via the Sign-In page and the Create Account link on the menu:
	   a. (TC1) Click the Sign-In link and verify that the system displays the Sign-In page. Click Create Account, and then verify that the system displays the Add Account Information page.
	   b. (TC2) Click the Create Account link and then verify that the system displays the Add Account Information page.
	2. At the Create Account page enter test case data TC3 and click the "Submit" button. Verify that the system displays the Verify Account page.
	3. Verify that the data on this page corresponds to test case data TC3, and click on the "Yes" button.
	4. Verify that you are signed in as "testbuyer10."

Expected final state of the system after the test case finishes	The Account Home page is displayed and contains the following string: *testbuyer10 signed in*.
Expected state of the data used by the system after the test case finishes	The system adds a record to the UserAccount table. The system adds a record to the CreditCard table. The system adds a record to the UserGroup table. Verify that the following query on the BooksREasy database returns one row with the columns matching the test case data TC3: SELECT ° FROM UserAccount, CreditCard, UserGroup WHERE CreditCard.UniqueId=UserAccount.UniqueId AND UserGroup.UniqueId=UserAccount.UniqueId AND UserAccount.UserId='<username>' where you replace <username> with the actual value of the username in the test case data; e.g., testbuyer10 for TC3 Also verify that in the returned row the GroupId column contains "Registered Buyer."

Create Account page enter test case data TC3/TCxyz and click the "Submit" button. Verify that the system displays the Verify Account page. The expected results are defined by each test case. But in general if the two test cases define different system environment and data states, it is easier to copy the test procedure and adapt its definition.

Test Coverage Matrix

Because there is only one test coverage matrix for all the system, Table 9-9 is an excerpt that presents only the implementation classes participating in the sequence diagrams for the use case scenario defining the basic flow of events. As a reminder, you need to consider the sequence diagrams of the design model, because this is the only model that references implementation classes. Notice that the UserGroupInfo class, which appears on the "Detail:Assign User to Group" sequence diagram (see Figure 6-27 in Chapter 6), is notably absent from the test coverage matrix. The reason is that this is a strongly typed DataSet class, thus it is considered an infrastructure class, which does not need to be assessed with any test case. To create this matrix you need to consider the sequence diagrams that correspond to the use case scenario covered by the referenced test cases. These diagrams were presented in Figures 6-23, 6-25, 6-26, and 6-27 in Chapter 6.

In Table 9-9 we can make the following remarks:

- CreateAccount_Entry class: Strictly considering the sequence diagrams, we cannot identify that InitializeComponent and OnInit are tested in the listed test cases. But because we know the way that .NET executes these operations, we also know that they are called before the Page_Load operation.

- CreateAccount_Entry class: Because the btnCancel_Click operation is not covered by any of the specified test cases, it should be covered by test cases corresponding to its use case scenario. Indeed, this operation relates to the "User Cancels Request" alternate flow of events for the Create Account use case.

- CreateAccount_Verify class: Same remark for the btnCancel_Click operation as in CreateAccount_Entry class.

Table 9-9: Test coverage matrix excerpt.

Class	Operation	Unit Test	TC1	TC2	TC3
CreateAccount_Entry	btnCancel_Click				
	btnSubmit_Click				X
	InitializeComponent		X	X	X
	IsCreditCardValid				X
	IsExpirationValid				X
	IsUserUnique				X
	OnInit		X	X	X
	Page_Load		X	X	X
CreateAccount_Verify	btnCancel_Click				
	btnYes_Click				X
	InitializeComponent				X
	OnInit				X
	Page_Load				X
Home_Account	InitializeComponent				X
	OnInit				X
	Page_Load				X
CreateAccountDispatcher	ProcessEvents				X
	ShowEntry				X
	ShowVerify				X
	SubmitEntry				X
	SumbitVerify				X
AccountManager	activateUserAccount				
	CreateAccount				X
	DeactivateUserAccount				
	GetCreditCardInfo				
	getCreditCardInfoByCardNumber				
	getUserAccountByUniqueId				
	GetUserAccountByUserId	X			X
	GetUserGroupByUniqueId				
	SetUserUIDToGroupId				X
	UpdateAccount				
	ValidateAccount				
CreditCardManager	chargeTransactionFee				
	IsCreditCardValid				X

Class	Operation	Unit Test	TC1	TC2	TC3
UserAccount	Create				X
	findByUserId				X
	findByUniqueId				
	Update				X
CreditCard	Create				X
	findByCardNumber				
	findByUniqueId				
	Update				X
UserGroup	Create				X
	findByUniqueId				
	Update				X

- CreateAccountDispatcher class: As its name implies, the operations of this class are very specific to the Create Account use case, so it should be no surprise that all its operations are covered by the selected test cases.

- AccountManager class: In contrast with CreateAccountDispatcher this is a general class, and this is the reason that only a few operations are covered by the selected test cases. Other test cases from other use case scenarios of the same or other use cases will need to cover the rest of the operations.

- CreditCardManager, CreditCard, and UserGroup: Same remark as for AccountManager class.

Unit Tests

In the test coverage matrix of the previous section, the only operation of implementation classes that is marked is getUserAccountByUserId, because, as a matter of conciseness, this is the only operation for which I will review the unit tests. In fact the stub and unit tests of the setUserUIDToGroupId operation have already been reviewed in Figures 9-2 and 9-3, respectively. In the stub definition of Figure 9-2 you can notice the test on the UserId argument. This test enables the support of the abnormal condition that occurs when the requested user account is not in the database. In this case, the specification of the operation is to return an empty DataSet. The actual code of the operation

```
namespace BooksREasy.UserAcctMgr.UserAcctMgrBLL
{
    using System;
    using BooksREasy.Common.UtilityClasses;
    using BooksREasy.UserAcctMgr.UserAcctMgrDAL.Stubs;

    public class AccountManager : MarshalByRefObject
        /// <summary>
        /// getUserAccountByUserId: Locates the user account with the specified userId.
        /// </summary>
        /// <param name="userId">userID of the user to retrieve user account information for.</param>
        /// <returns>Typed UserInfo dataset that contains the UserAccount record with a matching userID.</returns>
        public UserInfo getUserAccountByUserId (string userId)
        {
            return new UserAccount() .findByUserId(userId);
        }
}
```

Figure 9-4: Definition of the actual getUserAccountByUserId implementation class.

is presented in Figure 9-4, where the only difference with the definition of Figure 9-2 is that we have replaced the "TODO:" with the call to the findByUserId of the UserAccount class in the Data Access Layer (DAL).

In fact, as the UserAccount class defines another unit, the call is directed to the corresponding stub, thanks to the "using" close of the class definition. This is transparent to the developer, who can go about and code the operation definitions as though all the external units were already completed. Figure 9-5 presents the stub of this DAL class. You can notice that it has the same definition as the stub for the getUserAccountByUserId operation of the AccountManager class. This is sensible as the only thing that getUserAccountByUserId does is to delegate to findByUserId. Nevertheless, as explained in the Approach section, you cannot call the findByUserId stub from the getUserAccountByUserId stub.

The unit tests for the getUserAccountByUserId operation were presented in Figure 9-3, where you can notice in the fail_Invalid_UserId test how a cleverly coded stub can help you test various conditions.

Summary

In this chapter we reviewed the activities and artifacts related to the functional testing of the system. With these activities you produce six artifacts: test cases,

```
namespace BooksREasy.UserAcctMgr.UserAcctMgrDAL.Stubs
{
    using System;
    using BooksREasy.Common.UtilityClasses;

    public class UserAccount
    {
        public UserInfo findByUserId (string userId)
        {
            UserInfo dsUser = new UserInfo();
            if (userId=="testbuyer10")
            {
                dsUser.UserAccount.AddUserAccountRow(dsUser.UserAccount.NewUserAccountRow());
                dsUser.UserAccount[0].UserId=userID
                dsUser.UserAccount[0].Password="testbuyer10pwd";
                dsUser.UserAccount[0].Email="testbuyer10@softgnosis.com";
                dsUser.UserAccount[0].Addr1="1, High Street";
                dsUser.UserAccount[0].City="London";
                dsUser.UserAccount[0].Country="UK"
                dsUser.UserAccount[0].SecretNumber="1111";
                dsUser.UserAccount[0].State="";
                dsUser.UserAccount[0].Status=CommonKeyWords.ACTIVE;
                dsUser.UserAccount[0].Zip="W1";
            }
            return dsUser;
        }
```

Figure 9-5: Definition of the UserAccount stub and its findByUserId operation.

test procedures, test scenarios, test coverage matrix, unit stubs, and unit tests. Within this type of testing, we have specifically discussed the two stages of unit test and system test, with a focus on black box testing. Functional testing consists of asserting that the system operates according to its functional specifications as captured in the use cases. The cornerstone of functional testing is the test case, which corresponds to one use case scenario and represents one possible flow of events of a use case.

The test coverage matrix helps to validate that all the classes and all their operations are allocated to at least one test case, and that unit tests have been defined for each one. A complete validation uses a code coverage tool to verify that each class operation is actually exercised within the test case in which it is allocated. Test cases are used to build the test procedures, which need to be followed in order to execute the tests. Test cases can be compounded into test scenarios in order to represent and test complex user sessions on the system.

Unit tests are most likely to use a combination of white box and black box approaches. White box testing involves using debugger tools. In the black box approach to unit testing, you first systematically create stubs as soon as implementation classes and their operations are defined in the design model. These stubs are then accessible by all developers, who first create unit tests for the units they have responsibility for. Only then can developers start coding the implementation of each operation, using stubbed calls to external units that are not yet available.

Creating stubs and unit tests is also useful as an additional level of design, before starting to code the actual operations. When the unit implementation is complete, the unit tests will assess that the unit operates to its specifications. Using the .NET namespaces feature to your advantage, you can write code that you can easily integrate with just a change of the namespace referenced within the definition of an implementation class.

System tests take place at the end of the development iteration and consist of executing all the test cases of all the iterations before and including the current one. Regression testing is the act of repeating the execution of test cases that have passed in a previous iteration, in order to assert that the new development has not induced any defects in any part of the system previously tested. For this purpose, it is important to use automated testing tools to support the testing activities.

Chapter 10
Traceability at Work

Introduction

In the Introduction to Chapter 1, I gave much emphasis to the concept of traceability, and thereafter also in several places throughout the book. I have pointed to the main practical implication of this concept, which is to facilitate impact analysis; that is, identifying what has to be changed in response to a modification at any level of system specification.

During the course of the discussion I have presented the evolution of knowledge, represented as various artifacts, explaining the rationale for their existence and the approach in developing each one. In doing so I took great care to pinpoint the traceability paths in the following ways:

- Identifying the inputs used for the definition of each artifact. All artifacts are represented in the four process diagrams of Chapter 1, and by examining these diagrams it is easy to identify the inputs of each artifact.

- Defining traceability information as part of the artifact (where appropriate); e.g., in many of the diagrams of the various UML models. In this perspective it is interesting to note that I did use the specific stereotype of "trace" for the relationship between two model elements representing two different levels of abstraction.

- Presenting the techniques that help you link two artifacts to each other; e.g., how the .NET role-based security attributes in code link with the actor diagram, the use case model, and the sequence diagrams, through the role-based security matrix.

- Describing the contribution in term of traceability of the various tools that were presented: modeling tools like Rational XDE and Microsoft Visual Studio .NET

In this chapter I will show you how this mindset is put to good use, paying for the work done in defining and maintaining the traceability information. To achieve this I will take you through the study of a change request for a feature of the solution. Most of you are probably much too familiar with the situation where a change request looks so easy to implement that someone will jump on the code and make the changes. The next thing you know, you have to make changes in ten more places before the system operates correctly again.

In this chapter I will demonstrate how using traceability will help to correctly identify all artifacts that need to be changed, and in which way. For this, I will be using the four ways described above that help trace all artifacts back and forth. This is the first step that will enable the project manager to cost the change request in terms of time and people needed to implement it, henceforth in terms of financial cost for the project. Having established traceability paths through the process, I will show you how easy it is to do this costing in an accurate and timely manner. In turn this helps to ensure the success of the project in terms of maintaining quality, keeping within budget, and finishing on time.

The Scenario

Let's consider the following scenario. The project is in its Construction phase, specifically in the first iteration of that phase, where it was decided to complete the development of the User Account Management use cases. The iteration draws to its end, system testing is well under way, all the test cases have been exercised, and all have passed.

Meanwhile, in the client organization, a new project leader is taking over the responsibility of the project and is busy getting up to speed with the specifications, which define the system requirements, as agreed between the client and the development organizations. Specifically the project leader reviews the following artifacts: system vision, business glossary, business rules, business object model, system use case definitions and use case model, system glossary, scope map, and user experience model and associated screen mock-ups.

The project leader notices that in the specifications there is no provision for validation of the ZIP/Postal Code field of the user address. After discussing this detail with the user representatives, the client organization decides that it is worth adding some validation for that field. In keeping the discussion simple, I will assume that the only constraint is to validate that any ZIP Code for a U.S. address complies with the ZIP+4 code format (5 digits and optionally a dash followed with 4 more digits; e.g., 90048-4563), and any Postcode for a U.K. address follows the pattern of U.K. Postcodes (Outcode<space>Incode; e.g., TW13 7HR); see Table 10-1, where an "A" indicates an alphabetic character, an "N" indicates a numeric character, and "q" represents a space.

No constraints are imposed on Postal Code validation for other countries. This defines a change request that is communicated to the project manager and functional analyst of the development organization, who are asked to define a cost for that modification of the system specifications.

Let's consider the series of actions that the project manager has to take, in order to evaluate the impact of this modification on the system development, and hence be able to calculate its cost.

Table 10-1: U.K. Postcode formats.

Outcode	Incode	Example
AN	NAA	M1q1AA
ANN	NAA	M60q1NW
AAN	NAA	CR2q6XH
AANN	NAA	DN55q1PT
ANA	NAA	W1Pq1HQ
AANA	NAA	EC1Aq1BB

Impact Analysis

As noted in Chapter 1, the process is defined by the artifacts and activities needed to produce them. The artifacts are presented in the four process diagrams in Chapter 1, while the activities are described in the discussion throughout the book. In these diagrams you can easily identify the inputs for each artifact.

Therefore, conducting an impact analysis entails taking the following two steps:

- Identify the artifacts impacted by the changes.
- Knowing the activities needed to produce or maintain the corresponding artifacts, evaluate the cost in terms of time and resources needed to implement the changes.

Business Model

The first question that needs to be answered is where to document this new element of functional specification. The new constraint on the validation of the ZIP/Postal Code field is effectively defining a new business rule. Thus, the first step for the project manager is to consult with the functional analyst, who has to decide if this business rule should be documented in the business rules document or as part of the business glossary. In this case, as the ZIP/Postal Code field is part of the definition of the User Account business object, it makes more sense to attach the constraint to the business glossary. Hence, the first artifact needing to be modified is the business glossary.

Reviewing the process diagrams, and having the correct level of understanding of the activities of the process, the functional analyst and project leader can identify other artifacts that potentially need to be modified. One such artifact is the business object model, but in reality it does not need change, as we only modify the definition of an existing business object and do not add a new one.

Use Case Model

As this is a use case-driven process, any modification of the functional specification is likely to impact the use case definitions. The User Account business object is referenced in the following two use cases: Create Account and Manage Account. In these use cases, the "User Enters Invalid User Account Information" alternate flow does not explicitly discuss the situation of an invalid ZIP/Postal Code. Both of these use cases need to be amended in order to add details on this situation. As a consequence of a use case modification, we are also likely to identify changes or additions to test cases, which I will discuss later.

User Experience Model

The use cases are realized in the user experience model by UML collaboration elements, which are stereotyped "use case storyboard," as presented in Figure 10-1.

This diagram is a traceability aid and it helps identify the storyboard that might be impacted by the change. In our case, these will be the Create Account and Manage Account storyboards, as they realize the two use cases that had to be modified previously. But reviewing these artifacts, we cannot see any need for a change.

Another artifact in the user experience model that might need to be updated is the screen mock-up of the input form that is used to capture the

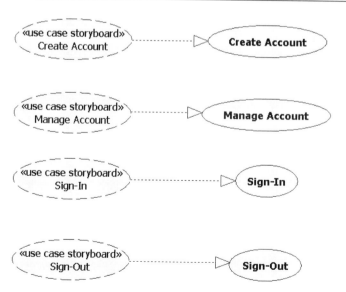

Figure 10-1: User Account Management storyboards.

User Account information, which is the "account info form." Note that the fact that both Manage Account and New Account screens use this input form hints that the resulting impact of the change on both use cases will result in only one change in some artifacts sitting downstream of the traceability path. Because we do not add a new field in the Create Account object, we do not need to add a new input field either, thus this form will need no change.

The important information that we gather from this step is that the change may affect an artifact that is traced back to the "account info form," which is used by both the above-identified storyboards, as we can find by examining the participants diagrams of these storyboards (see Figure 4-6, in Chapter 4, for the participants diagram of the Create Account storyboard).

Analysis Model

We also know that the business object model constitutes the principal input for the definition of the managed entities in the analysis model. But because we do not add any new entity, the entity definitions will not need to change either, as these definitions do not hold any information on the fields of the entities. Instead, the definitions of the fields are carried over from the glossaries to the design model (specifically the data model).

The use cases are realized in the analysis model by UML elements of type collaboration and stereotyped "Use Case Realization," as presented in Figure 10-2.

Similar to Figure 10-1, this diagram is a traceability aid, and it helps identify the use case realizations that might be impacted by the change. In our case, these will be the Create Account and Manage Account use case realizations, as they realize the two use cases that had to be modified previously. Considering the Create Account use case realization, we first need to review its participants diagram, shown in Figure 10-3.

We have already discussed the impact on the User Account entity, but we notice on this diagram the boundary classes. Thus, we should consider the boundary traceability diagram for User Account Management, presented in Figure 10-4.

In this diagram we can notice that the "New Account" and "Manage Account" boundary classes both trace back to two user experience screens that both contain the "account info form" identified previously. This means that we have to consider, downstream in the traceability path, any artifact that traces back to these two boundary classes.

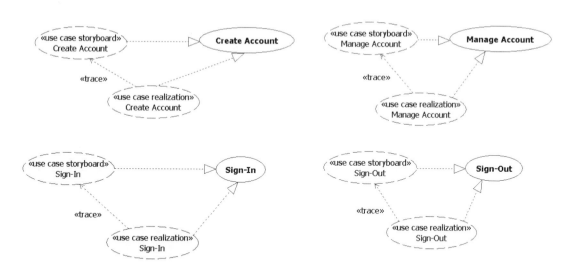

Figure 10-2: Realizations diagram.

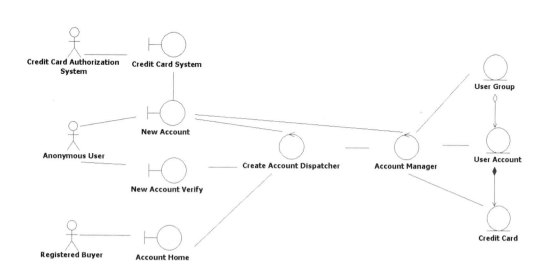

Figure 10-3: View Of Participating Classes diagram for the Create Account use case.

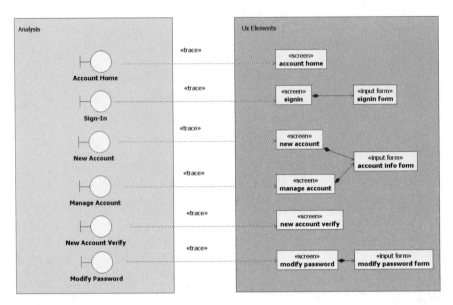

Figure 10-4: Tracing boundary classes to screens for the User Account Management package.

Sequence diagrams are central to this process; hence, it is always equally important to consider the sequence diagrams of the analysis and design models in order to evaluate the impact of a modification. In the rest of the discussion I will consider only the Create Account use case, but in reality you would also review the Manage Account use case, as it is also impacted by the change. The diagram in Figure 10-5 presents the basic flow for the Create Account use case realization.

In this diagram we can notice that the validation of the user input, on the "New Account" boundary class, is handled by the class itself (message number 3 on the diagram: "validate user account information"). This information confirms the previous conclusion that we shall need to carefully review the realization of this boundary class in the implementation model (and henceforth in the code). To do this we need to find the appropriate traceability information in the design model.

Here we enter the realm of the software architect, who needs to be consulted on the impact of design and implementation artifacts, due to changes on

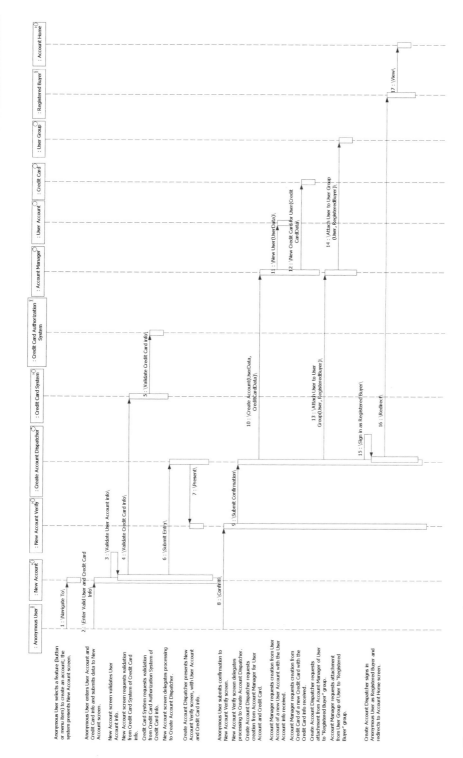

Figure 10-5: Sequence diagram for the Create Account use case.

227

the artifacts identified so far. Note, however, that the software architect may as well be involved from the beginning of the impact analysis, along with the functional architect and the project manager, in a joint session on change request evaluations.

Data Model

The business object definition is used as input to the data model. But because there is no new field definition (ZIP/Postal Code is already defined), there will be no change in the definition of the User Account table. One possible change would be a database integrity constraint that enforces the business rule. In reality the selected architecture mechanisms do not enforce this type of constraint in the database, but instead, as seen in the analysis model, a boundary class handles the validation of the input form.

Design Model

Similar to the analysis model, we need to review the use case realizations of the design model. To correctly identify the impacted use cases we will use the traceability diagram of Figure 10-6, which is similar to Figures 10-1 and 10-2.

From this diagram we identify that the two use case realizations that are of interest in the design model are "Create Account" and "Manage Account," as these are tracing back to the two corresponding use case realizations in the analysis model impacted by the change.

Reviewing the sequence diagrams associated with these use case realizations, we notice in the "CreateAccount_Entry validation" diagram presented in Figure 10-7 that the validation operation, identified previously in the analysis model, is implemented by the CreateAccount_Entry implementation class.

Considering the "Boundary Traceability (Mapping)" diagram in Figure 10-8, we get confirmation that this implementation class traces back to the "New Account" boundary class of the analysis model, which was identified previously to be in the traceability path of the impacted artifacts.

As a general note, other elements of the design model that can also be used as traceability aids are the participants diagrams of the various layers as well as any traceability diagram created during the design.

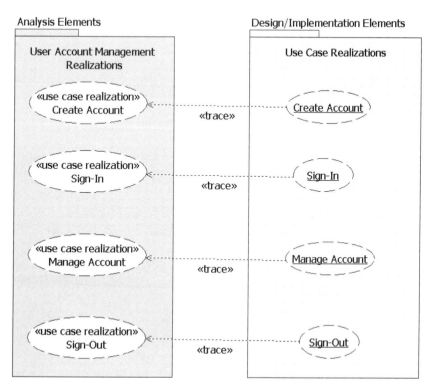

Figure 10-6: Tracing use case realizations from design to analysis.

Implementation Model, Test Cases, and Code

Having established which implementation classes will be impacted by the change, we also need to define how they will be affected. We will take advantage of the same architecture mechanism used for the validation of other input fields, as presented in the sequence diagram of Figure 10-7. This mechanism is the ASP.NET custom validator Web control. From this diagram we can see that we need to define a new validation operation (e.g., IsZip_PostCodeValid in the CreateAccount_Entry implementation class). This operation will be called by the btnSubmit_Click operation. Following the ASP.NET pattern, we also need to add a custom validator control on the associated Web control, which should delegate the validation to the IsZip_PostCodeValid validation

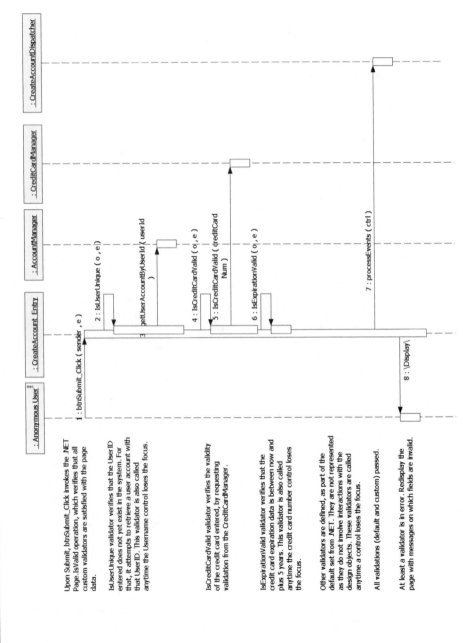

The following describes the sequence of events and validations shown in the diagram:

Upon Submit, btnSubmit_Click invokes the .NET Page.IsValid operation, which verifies that all custom validators are satisfied with the page data.

IsUserUnique validator verifies that the UserID entered does not yet exist in the system. For that, it attempts to retrieve a user account with that UserID. This validator is also called anytime the Username control loses the focus.

IsCreditCardValid validator verifies the validity of the credit card entered, by requesting validation from the CreditCardManager.

IsExpirationValid validator verifies that the credit card expiration data is between now and plus 5 years. This validator is also called anytime the credit card number control loses the focus.

Other validators are defined, as part of the default set from .NET. They are not represented as they do not involve interactions with the design objects. These validators are called anytime a control loses the focus.

All validations (default and custom) passed.

At least a validator is in error. Redisplay the page with messages on which fields are invalid.

Figure 10-7: Collaboration detail: CreateAccount_Entry validation.

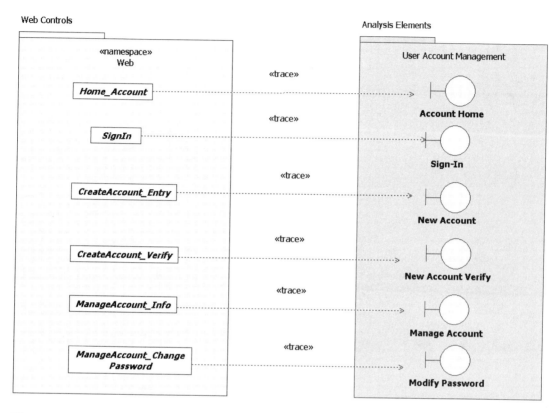

Figure 10-8: Tracing Web forms/controls to analysis classes.

operation. As a result, both CreateAccount_Entry.ascx and CreateAccount_Entry.ascx.cs will need to be modified.

Continuing the impact analysis, the change identified in the implementation class will in turn impact some sequence diagrams where this class is used, particularly the "CreateAccount_Entry validation" diagram of Figure 10-7 above. In that diagram we will need to represent the newly defined operation.

In turn the changes in the sequence diagram will result in modifications or additions of test cases. Indeed, as explained in Chapters 3, 5, and 9, the sequence diagrams represent use case scenarios that are exercised by test cases. As hinted above, any change in a use case will likely impact the associated test cases. In the example of the ZIP/Postal Code change, this will result in additional test cases testing normal and abnormal conditions on the combination of the Country and ZIP/Postal Code. These test cases will complement the test cases TC4, TC5, and TC6 presented in Chapter 9.

Any change in the sequence diagrams should also be evaluated for its impact on the test coverage and role-based security matrixes. Indeed, in our case, we have defined a new operation on an implementation class that potentially needs to be listed in these two matrixes. The role-based security matrix will need to be reviewed in light of the new sequence diagrams for a possible change in security settings. In our situation, there will be no change to the role-based security matrix, because the security for a Web control class is attached to the class and not to its operations, as described in Chapter 8. But the test coverage matrix will need to be updated and will be used to ensure that unit tests and test cases are developed for the newly defined operation.

Note that a change in the code of an implementation class will result in the need to change the corresponding stub code. In doing so, the developers will get inspiration from the newly defined test cases, as discussed in Chapter 9. In the case of the ZIP/Postal Code change request, because the implementation class is a Web control, we do not use stubs, due to the complexity in developing them, as described in Chapter 9. Instead we would use a white box approach in testing with a Web control, that is, use of a code debugger.

Finally, any change in the implementation code has an impact on the unit tests defined for that code, as described in Chapter 9.

Summary

In this chapter we have identified the following artifacts that need to be modified in response to the change request received, along with the way they need to be changed:

- Business glossary: Add a constraint on the description of the ZIP/Postal Code field.
- Create Account and Manage Account use cases: Add details related to invalid ZIP/Postal Code.
- CreateAccount_Entry implementation class:

❏ In the code-behind class (CreateAccount_Entry.ascx.cs): Add a new validation operation—e.g., IsZip_PostCodeValid—that applies a specific regular expression depending on the country selected (U.S.: "\d{5}(-\d{4})?"; U.K.: "([a-zA-Z]{1,2}\\d{1,2}|[a-zA-Z]{1,2}\\d{1}[a-zA-Z])\\s\\d{1}[a-zA-Z]{2}"; no validation for other countries).

❏ In the Web control: Add a new custom validator, attached to the ZIP/Postal Code input field, and that points to the operation IsZip_PostCodeValid of the code-behind class.

■ "CreateAccount_Entry validation" sequence diagram: Represent the new validation operation.

■ Test cases: Create a new test case, similar to TC4, TC5, and TC6 of Chapter 9.

■ Test coverage matrix: Add a new entry for the IsZip_PostCodeValid of CreateAccount_Entry.

■ Unit tests: Amend the unit tests located in the CreateAccount_Entry.ascx.cs code file.

Knowing exactly what has to be done, it is now easy for the project manager, with input from the functional analyst and the software architect, to evaluate what resources are needed to implement the change, and how much time this will take. Then, the project manager can apply the information from the hourly rates table to calculate the cost of the change request.

Appendix A
Future Vision

The objective of this book is to educate practitioners about a software engineering discipline, which will be fundamental to prepare them for the next evolution of software development. This appendix describes my view of this evolution and points out the need for software engineering practices. Optimistically, I'll put a time frame of five years for the completion of the whole vision, although some elements are already maturing now.

Component-based systems are clearly the future of software engineering. .NET and J2EE are two component technologies that are meant to coexist. Developing a system will be a matter of mixing and matching off-the-shelf functionality that will be found in specialized functional packages. These packages already exist, but most of them lack the following elements:

- Integration with the application server. We currently have a strong push from product vendors to integrate their products with either .NET or J2EE.
- UML models of the product. These models will be integrated into the model of the new software. Thus modeling a new system will consist of integrating the models of the products that support the different functional areas of the solution with some specific modeling that will, in par-

ticular, glue all the submodels together. These models will come as patterns described in UML and probably in an XMI format.

- The ultimate element that we have to expect from the product vendors is a set of use cases to be integrated with the specification of the new software system. I was confronted with this situation in a project where I needed to integrate chat features with the solution. Our analysts developed a set of use cases, but the decision was made to use an off-the-shelf product. Obviously there wasn't a one-to-one match between the product features and the use cases. In an ideal world, the sensible thing to do would have been to agree with the client on the packaged solution and then on use cases that match the product features. Meanwhile, a certain level of effort was lost in defining these use cases. The ultimate convenience would have been to receive the use cases as part of the product, integrate them as part of the specifications in the solution, without the need to redefine use cases that would match the package features. In the future, I expect product vendors will propose use case patterns that can be integrated with the system specification.

So putting all this together, let's spell out a scenario of software development in five years:

- Requirements definitions, functional and nonfunctional. Functional elements will drive the package selection, while nonfunctional requirements will drive the platform selection.
- Choose an application server platform, either .NET or J2EE. Differentiation will be based on the following (from most important to least important criteria and based on a greenfield situation; this is a partial list covering the most important elements):
    - Availability of integrated functional packages (as described above).
    - Completeness of application services: queued components, loosely coupled events, messaging, application adaptors framework, and so on.
    - Platform robustness: security, scalability, and resilience.
    - Total cost of ownership (acquisition and maintenance). This will mainly be driven by the availability of skilled professionals.

- System specification by integrating use cases from product vendors and developing system-specific use cases.
- UML modeling of the solution by integrating UML models from product vendors and developing system-specific model elements.
- Generation of code for the specific application server. The modeling tool should have intimate integration with the application server.

In summary, in the very near future, the value-added products will be functional component suites that can quickly be integrated into new applications. These components would comply with a specific application framework architecture and could be made available as Web services. They will come as packages composed of:

- Use cases and cases studies.
- UML diagrams covering the test cases and usage pattern.
- Components as application framework-specific components (.NET or J2EE) or Web service interface specifications (including the service access details and Service Level Agreement).

Appendix B

BooksREasy Vision

This appendix describes the vision for the BooksREasy system. It discusses key terms and concepts, the problem the system addresses, its stakeholders and users, its features, and its functional and development constraints.

BooksREasy is an online bookstore. It is aimed at creating a new sales channel for the BooksREasy organization. This channel is specifically the Internet; it targets all customers who are conversant with the Internet and would appreciate the convenience to buy books at any time, anywhere.

The objective of the current effort is to quickly enable the organization to generate revenue from this channel, and the focus of the system will be to give customers the basic capability to browse the book catalogue and place orders. In a second dimension, the current effort will result in a software system that employs state-of-the-art design to ensure further extensibility. It should also result in a robust, secure system that supports the expected initial load, as further specified below.

Problem Statement

BooksREasy seeks to provide a secure environment where customers can browse the book catalogue and place orders for books. Specifically:

- Buyers need access to a large, diverse catalogue of books. The book catalogue should be organized into categories, although only one level of categorization is sufficient.

- Buyers should be able to select a list of books to buy (and for each book, to specify a different quantity). The Buyer should be able to modify the list of books selected and the quantities to order. When placing an order, the order should pertain to the list of selected books as a whole.

- Buyers need the option of remaining anonymous until they decide to place the order.

- BooksREasy must provide a secure environment for the customers to order books, and the administrator can effectively manage the customer accounts by deleting inactive accounts.

Stakeholders and Users

The major stakeholders and users of an online bookstore system are listed and described briefly in Table B-1. The next section provides additional information on their concerns and responsibilities.

In addition to the users described in this table, a casual (nonregistered) visitor to the bookstore site can browse the book catalogue, select books into a cart, and update the cart (but must assume the role of a Buyer before being allowed to place an order).

The functional features of BooksREasy (listed in the next section) are not unique and are likely to be found in most bookstore systems. The special requirements of this solution are nonfunctional, addressing the concerns of the bookstore site owner and bookstore system developer: ease and cost of development, security, extensibility, maintainability, and reuse. These concerns are met through the following:

- Rigorous use of software development best practices, including:
  - Requirements modeling.
  - Architecture and design modeling.
  - Round-trip engineering of the code from the design model.
  - System decomposition into business components.
- Use of .NET development framework.

Table B-1: Stakeholders and their responsibilities.

Stakeholder/User	Description	Concerns and Responsibilities
Buyer	An individual or an organization that orders books	Registers with the bookstore and provides a proof of credit
		Browses the catalogue of books
		Places an order for one or more books
		Pays using a registered credit card
		Maintains the account information
Bookstore site owner	An individual or an organization that owns the bookstore site	Defines, reviews, and accepts key requirements for the online bookstore system
		Maintains the catalogue of books to be displayed on the site
		Accepts book orders from the site and fulfills the orders
		Receives statistics of site usage, performance, and so on
		Assumes financial responsibility for management and development
Bookstore site administrator	An individual who administers the operations of the bookstore site	Monitors bookstore site activities and collects statistics
		Browses user accounts, updates user information (in particular the information that is collected by the system), and deactivates or deletes information
Bookstore system developer	An individual and/or organization that develops and maintains the BooksREasy online system	Understands the requirements of the system and satisfies the needs of the system stakeholders (Bookstore site owner in particular)
		Develops an elegant, well-architected, secure, maintainable, and extensible system
		Is able to reuse known solutions during the development of the system
		Is able to reuse system designs and parts in the subsequent development of similar systems

Features

The major features to be incorporated into BooksREasy are as follows:

Managing User Accounts

Bookstore site users (the Buyers) should be able to create accounts with the system and update account information if it is incorrect or if it changes.

The bookstore Administrator should be able to browse user accounts, update user information (in particular the information that is collected by the system), and deactivate or delete information.

Browsing a Structured Catalogue of Books and Placing Orders

Any user should be able to browse a catalogue of books organized into categories, read book descriptions, add book items into a cart, and update the cart quantities (including removing items from the cart). Registered Buyers should be able to place an order for the books contained in their cart.

Maintaining System Security

The system should support system security; in particular, it should:

- Authenticate users.
- Make sure that the users are allowed to perform only the operations for which they have authorization. This means that the system should check if a user belongs to a group that is authorized to perform a specific operation or even if an individual user should be allowed to perform certain operations. For example, an unregistered user should not be able to place an order; a Buyer should not be able to delete their account.

Functional Constraints

There is one particularly important constraining assumption that we need to address. It has to do with how the system takes the payment for an order. Upon registration, a Buyer has to enter credit card information to be used for the payments of orders. When placing an order, the system uses the credit card information attached to the Buyer's account to take payment of the order.

As a result, BooksREasy does not have to support the capture of credit card information upon checkout, as is common in other online commerce sites. However, such functionality should be easy to add by taking advantage of the very extensible structure of the system design.

Deployment Constraints

BooksREasy should be deployed on a Microsoft .NET deployment environment.

The application should be developed using the Rational product suite and Microsoft Visual Studio .NET and should follow the best practices described in the SoftGnosis Practical Process. In particular the development should produce all the key artifacts prescribed by the process:

- Documentation (system vision, glossaries, use case descriptions, test cases, and test procedures).
- Models (use case model, user experience model, analysis model, data model, design model, and implementation models).
- Code (source code, deployment descriptors, database scripts, etc.).

Appendix C
BooksREasy User Stories

This appendix collects the texts of the user stories, describing in a simple and nonformal way what the system is expected to do. Use the standard wordings of "Description of the Featured User" and "Description of What Happens" to orient the thinking of the users writing these descriptions.

Create Account

Description of the Featured User

The user is any individual who has accessed the BooksREasy Web site and does not have an account on the system. A user like this can browse the catalogue and select books to order, but cannot place orders. The unregistered individual wants to register because they want to be able to place orders or, when they try to place a first order, they are prompted to register first.

Description of What Happens

The user navigates to the BooksREasy Web site. The site should have a feature that indicates to the user that it supports registration. The user selects that feature, and the system should present the user with a registration form where they must enter the following information:

- Username
- Password
- E-mail address
- Credit card information:
  - Name on credit card
  - Card number
  - Card type
  - Card expiration date
- Billing address information:
  - Street address
  - City
  - State
  - ZIP/Postcode
  - Country

The user validates the input and the system has to create the account. Situations where the system should reject the account creation are

- The username already exists in the system.
- The credit card is not valid.
- Some item of information is missing.

Manage Account

Description of the Featured User

The user is any individual who has an account on the system and wants to modify some of its account information.

Description of What Happens

The user navigates to the BooksREasy Web site. The site should have a feature to allow the user to modify his or her account information. The user selects that feature and is presented with a form containing the current information on the account, where every item of information can be modified.

The user validates the input, and the system has to modify the account. Situations where the system should reject the account modification are

- The username is already an existing username in the system.
- The credit card is not a valid credit card.
- Some item of information is missing.

Sign-In

Description of the Featured User

The user is any individual who has an account on the system and wants to be authenticated by the system to have access to every system feature.

Description of What Happens

The user navigates to the BooksREasy Web site. The site should have a feature to allow the user to sign in to his or her account. The user selects that feature and is presented with a form prompting for his or her username and password. The user enters and validates the input, and if the system authenticates the user, it has to present him or her with all additional features available for a registered user. Situations where the system should reject the request for authentication include

- The username is not an existing username in the system.
- The password is invalid for the username entered.

Sign-Out

Description of the Featured User

The user is any individual who has an account on the system and is currently signed in. The user wants to return to an unauthenticated state, in order to quit the application with the assurance that his or her account is not accessible anymore.

Description of What Happens

The user is currently signed in to the BooksREasy Web site. The site should have a feature available at any time, to allow the user to sign out of the site. The user selects that feature, and the system has to present the user with the site's home page for an unauthenticated user.

Browse Catalogue

Description of the Featured User

The user is any individual who wants to buy books on the BooksREasy Web site. The user wants to browse the books available in the catalogue.

Description of What Happens

The user has accessed the BooksREasy Web site. The site should have a feature that gives the user access to the book catalogue. When the user selects that feature, he or she is given the choice to either select a category (each book is attached to only one category) or type in a search criteria, requesting the system to search for the books that match the criteria. The search criteria available shall be the following:

- Author
- Title
- ISBN
- Keyword (that is, any word in the book description)

In both cases the system should return a list of books, presenting for each book the title and the price. From this list the user must have access to a feature that allows him or her to select a book and review the following details:

- Title
- Author(s)

- Publisher
- Date published
- ISBN
- Price
- Description

Review Shopping Cart

Description of the Featured User

The user is any individual who wants to buy books on the BooksREasy Web site. The user has selected some book items in the shopping cart. The user wants to review the shopping cart in order to amend ordered quantities or remove items.

Description of What Happens

The user has accessed the BooksREasy Web site. The site should have a feature available at any time that gives the user access to the shopping cart. When the user selects that feature, he or she is presented with the shopping cart:

- Quantity for each item
- Book title for each item
- Unit price for each item
- Total price for each item (quantity X unit price)
- Total price for the order (sum of total price of each item)

The user can modify the quantities of each book item in the cart. When the user validates the modifications, the system should recalculate the totals. If the user sets the quantity of an item to 0, the system should remove that item from the cart. Situations where the system should reject the requested modifications include the following:

- The user input does not represent a zero or positive integer number.

Check-Out

Description of the Featured User

The user is any individual who wants to buy books on the BooksREasy Web site. The user has selected some book items in the shopping cart. The user wants to place an order for the contents of the shopping cart.

Description of What Happens

The user has accessed the BooksREasy Web site and is reviewing his or her shopping cart. At any time when there are items in the cart, the site should provide a feature to proceed to checkout. When the user selects that feature, provided the user is signed in, he or she is presented with an order summary form containing the list of book items from the shopping cart:

- Quantity for each item
- Book title for each item
- Unit price for each item
- Total price for each item (quantity X unit price)
- Total price for the order (sum of total price of each item)

The user cannot modify any item of information. If the user is satisfied with the order summary, he or she can validate the order. The system validates and debits the credit card that is on file for the user, and generates an order number that is presented to the user as confirmation of placing the order.

In the case that the user is not signed in, the system should not proceed to the order summary form, but instead invite the user to sign in before resuming the checkout.

Manage Users

Description of the Featured User

The user is any individual who has administrative privileges. The user wants to deactivate a user account.

Description of What Happens

The user has accessed the BooksREasy Web site and has been authenticated as an Administrator. The site should provide a feature to deactivate accounts. This feature should be accessible only to users who are signed in and are part of the Administrator group. When the user selects that feature, they are given the choice to either select a username from a list of all usernames of the system or type in a search criteria, requesting the system to search for the user accounts that match the criteria. The search criteria available will be any combination of the following:

- Username
- E-mail address
- Billing address (any word in the address)
- ZIP/Postcode

In both cases the system should return a list of user accounts, presenting for each account the username and e-mail. From this list the user must have access to a feature that allows him or her to select a user account for deactivation. The system should then present the user with a form asking confirmation of the deactivation and present the following account details:

- Username
- E-mail
- Billing address

Appendix D

User Account Management Use Cases

Appendix D collects the texts for the use cases for the User Accounts Management Package.

Name	Create Account
Brief Description	The Create Account use case allows the User to create and activate an account, which contains information about the User.
	Upon successful account creation, the User is also signed in.
	The User is created with a role of Registered Buyer.
Actor(s)	Anonymous User
Flow of Events	
Basic Flow	

This use case starts when the User accesses the Create Account feature of the system.

1. The system displays the *User Account* information that needs to be entered for the User.
2. The User enters the required *User Account* information values and requests that the system save the entered values. The system validates the *User Account* data entered by the User.
3. The system also validates the *Credit Card* by submitting a *Credit Card* validation request to the Credit Card Authorization System.
4. The system then displays the entered data and asks the User to confirm that an account should be created with the entered values.
5. The User confirms that an account should be created. A new account is created and activated for the User. The *User Account* data provided is stored in the User's new account. The system also assigns the User to the group of Registered Buyers, and stores this information in relation to the User Account.

6. The system signs in the User under the newly created account. The system notifies the User that their account has been activated and that the new values have been saved.

7. The use case ends.

Alternate Flows

Title	Description
User Cancels Request	At any time, the User may choose to cancel the current operation. If the User cancels during account creation, the account is not created.
User Enters Invalid User Account Information	If the system determines that the User entered invalid *User Account* information, the following occurs:

- The system describes what data was invalid and presents the User with suggestions for entering valid data.
- The system prompts the User to re-enter the *User Account* information.
- The User re-enters the information and the system revalidates it.
- If valid information is entered, the *User Account* information is stored.
- If invalid data is entered, the "User Enters Invalid User Account Information" alternative flow is executed again. This repeats until valid information is entered or until the User cancels the Create Account request.

Invalid *User Account* information:

- Missing information items
- Username already exists in the system
- *User Account* information entered does not comply with its definition in the glossary
- Not well-formed e-mail address
- *Credit card* is not valid
- Offending words in any part of the *User Account* information

Pre-Conditions

Title	Description
None	

Post-Conditions

Title	Description
Success	The *User Account* was created and activated, and the User is signed in as a role of Registered Buyer.
The User Account Was Not Created	This occurs when the User fails to enter valid *User Account* data or if the User chooses to cancel the Create Account request. In such a case, the account is not created.

Extension Points

None

Name	Manage Account
Brief Description	The Manage Account use case allows the User to update the User Account Information maintained in the User's account.
Actor(s)	*Registered User:* Registered Buyer, Admin

Flow of Events

Basic Flow

This use case starts when the User accesses the system feature that enables him or her to update the information that is maintained in the User's account.

1. The system displays the *User Account* information currently stored for the User.
2. The User enters the desired *User Account* information values and requests that the system save the entered values.
3. The system validates the entered *User Account* information.
4. The system also validates the *Credit Card* by submitting a *Credit Card* validation request to the Credit Card Authorization System.
5. The values for the *User Account* information are stored in the User's account. The system notifies the User that the account has been updated.
6. The use case ends.

Alternate Flows

Title	Description
User Cancels Request	At any time, the User may choose to cancel the account update/deactivation. At which point the processing is discontinued, the User Account remains unchanged, and the User is notified that the account management request has been cancelled.
User Enters Invalid User Account Information	If during Modify Account, the system determines that the User entered invalid *User Account* information, the following occurs: 1. The system describes which entered data was invalid and presents the User with suggestions for entering valid data. 2. The system prompts the User to re-enter the invalid information. 3. The User re-enters the information and the system revalidates it. 4. If valid information is entered, the User Account information is stored. 5. If invalid information is entered, the "User Enters Invalid User Account Information" alternative flow is executed again. This continues until the User enters valid information or chooses Cancel (see the "User Cancels Account Management Request" alternative flow). Invalid *User Account* information: ■ Missing information items ■ Username already exists in the system

- *User Account* information entered does not comply with its definition in the glossary
- Not well-formed e-mail address
- *Credit card* is not valid
- Offending words in any part of the *User Account* information

Pre-Conditions

Title	Description
User Is Signed In	The User must be signed in before the User can edit or deactivate their account. See the Sign-In use case.

Post-Conditions

Title	Description
Success	The User-entered data is stored in the User Account.
The User Account Was Not Updated	The User entered invalid data or chose to cancel the account management request. In either case, there is no change to the User Account.

Extension Points

None

Name	Sign-In
Brief Description	The Sign-In use case allows the User to authenticate him or herself to the system and obtain access to all features of the role he or she is associated with as defined in their User Account.
	If the User does not have an account in the system, the User is given the opportunity to create a new User Account. See the **Create Account** use case.
Actor(s)	Anonymous User

Flow of Events

Basic Flow

This use case starts when the User accesses the sign-in feature of the system.

1. The system prompts the User for his or her username and password.
2. The User enters his or her username and password.
3. The system validates the entered information, making sure that the entered username and password are valid for one User Account in the system, and that the required password is entered for the entered username.
4. The User is signed in. The system displays a message indicating that the User is signed in.
5. The use case ends.

Alternate Flows

Title	Description
New User	If the User does not have an account, the system will give the User the opportunity to create an account. See the **Create Account** use case. Once the account is created, the User is considered signed in.
User Fails Authentication	If the User entered an invalid username and/or password, the following occurs: 1. The system describes the reasons why the User failed authentication. 2. The system presents the User with suggestions for changes necessary to allow the User to pass authentication. 3. The system prompts the User to re-enter the invalid information. 4. The Basic Flow continues where the User enters new information (see Step 2 of the Basic Flow)

Pre-Conditions

Title	Description
None	

Post-Conditions

Title	Description
Success	The User is authenticated and the system displays all features available for the role the User is associated with as defined in their User Account.
User Not Signed In	This can occur because the User repeatedly entered invalid sign-in information. The User has been notified of the reason why he or she were not signed in. The User is not authenticated and remains in the Anonymous User role.

Extension Points

None

Bibliography

Practical Bibliography

Kurt Bittner and Ian Spence, *Use Case Modeling*. Addison-Wesley, 2003.

Jim Conallen, *Building Web Applications with UML (Second Edition)*. Addison-Wesley, 2003.

Martin Fowler and Kendall Scott, *UML Distilled, Second Edition*. Addison-Wesley, 2000.

Jim Heumann, "Generating Test Cases From Use Cases," *The Rational Edge*, June 1999.

Ivar Jacobson, Maria Ericsson, and Agneta Jacobson, *The Object Advantage—Business Process Reengineering with Object Technology*. Addison-Wesley, 1995.

Philippe Kruchten, *The Rational Unified Process: An Introduction, Second Edition*. Addison-Wesley, 2000.

Eric J. Naiburg and Robert A. Maksimchuk, *UML for Database Design*. Addison-Wesley, 2002.

Doug Rosenberg and Kendall Scott, *Use Case Driven Object Modeling with UML: A Practical Approach*. Addison-Wesley, 1999.

Doug Rosenberg and Kendall Scott, *Applying Use Case Driven Object Modeling with UML: An Annotated e-Commerce Example*. Addison-Wesley, 2001.

David A. Sykes and John D. McGregor, *A Practical Guide to Testing Object-Oriented Software*. Addison-Wesley, 2001.

Extended Bibliography

Kent Beck, *Extreme Programming Explained: Embrace Change*. Addison-Wesley, 2000.

Robert V. Binder, *Testing Object-Oriented Systems*. Addison-Wesley, 2000.

Desmond Francis D'Souza and Alan Cameron Wills, *Objects, Components, and Frameworks with UML: The Catalysis Approach*. Addison-Wesley, 1999.

Ivar Jacobson, Magnus Christerson, Patrik Jonsson, and Gunnar Övergaard, *Object-Oriented Software Engineering: A Use Case Driven Approach*. Addison-Wesley, 1992.

Magnus Penker and Hans-Erik Eriksson, *Business Modeling with UML: Business Patterns at Work*. John Wiley & Sons, 2000.

Bruce Schneier, *Secrets and Lies: Digital Security in a Networked World*. John Wiley & Sons, 2000.

John Viega and Gary McGraw, *Building Secure Software: How to Avoid Security Problems the Right Way*. Addison-Wesley, 2002.

Jos B. Warmer and Anneke G. Kleppe, *The Object Constraint Language:Precise Modeling with UML*. Addison-Wesley, 1999.

.NET Essential Bookshelf

F. Scott Barker, *Database Programming with Visual Basic .NET and ADO.NET: Tips, Tutorials, and Code.* Sams, 2002.

David Chappell, *Understanding .NET: A Tutorial and Analysis.* Addison-Wesley, 2002.

Brian A. LaMacchia, Sebastian Lange, Matthew Lyons, Rudi Martin, and Kevin T. Price, *.NET Framework Security.* Addison-Wesley, 2002.

Jesse Liberty, *Programming C#.* O'Reilly, 2002.

Jeffrey Richter, *Applied Microsoft .NET Framework Programming.* Microsoft Press, 2002.

Stephen Walther, *ASP.NET Unleashed.* Sams, 2002.

Index